ECHOES ON THE LAKE

ECHOES ON THE LAKE

The Common Loon in Poetry

MARIA M.

Mohammed Altaf Hussain

CONTENTS

INDEX

INTRODUCTION

In the quietude of a northern lake, where undulating waters reflect the material of an immaculate sky, an enchanted presence graces the scene — the Normal Nut case. Its frightful calls resound through the tranquility, winding around an ethereal song that reverberates with the spirit. In the domain of verse, this baffling bird arises as a dream, rousing sections that navigate the fragile limit between nature's excellence and the human experience. Welcome to the universe of "Reverberations on the Lake: The Normal Nut case in Verse," an investigation that discloses the immortal exchange between avian beauty, beautiful articulation, and the unpredictable woven artwork of our association with the regular world.

1. **Setting the Stage: The Normal Nut case's Persona**
   Prior to digging into the lovely scene, fathoming the embodiment of the Normal Loon is fundamental. Deductively known as Gavia immer, this waterbird encapsulates polish with its smooth high contrast plumage. Nonetheless, its charm stretches out past the visual; it lives in the eerie calls that penetrate the quietness of lakeshores, making a hear-able orchestra that reverberations across the water's surface. The Normal Nut case, with its occasional relocations and unmistakable ways of behaving, becomes a bird as well as a living epitome of nature's verse.

2. **Verse as a Door to the Superb**
   At the core of this investigation lies the conviction that verse fills in as a course to the superb, a method for unwinding the secrets of the regular world. The Normal Nut case, with its lone floats and soul-blending calls, turns into an image of the untamed magnificence that artists try to catch in words. In the stanzas committed to the nut case, perusers are welcome to leave on an excursion that rises above the unremarkable, digging into the significant and slippery features of the avian domain.

3. **The Ageless Crossing point: Nature, Verse, and Human Experience**

The Normal Nut case, as a wonderful subject, enlightens the harmonious connection between nature, verse, and the human experience. Every refrain devoted to the nut case turns into a string that winds around together the normal world and the complex embroidery of human feelings. This investigation plans to unwind the interconnectedness of these components, exhibiting how the Normal Crackpot turns into a vessel through which writers express the unspeakable and perusers track down reverberation with the heartbeat of the Earth.

II. The Confounding Charms of the Normal Crackpot

1. **Tasteful Excellence as Motivation**

   The plumage of the Normal Crackpot, differentiating highly contrasting, structures a characteristic range that writers plunge into to paint clear pictures. Its smoothness in development across the water's surface turns into a dance, a living verse that spellbinds the onlooker's look. Artists, enlivened by the tasteful appeal of the crackpot, make sections that intend to catch its actual magnificence as well as the quintessence of polish that characterizes its presence.

2. **Tormenting Calls: A Sonic Embroidery**

   The spirit mixing calls of the Normal Nut case make a sonic embroidery that resounds through lakes and woodlands. In verse, these calls become more than simple sounds; they are ethereal tunes that bring out a scope of feelings. The eerie nature of the crackpot's voice motivates artists to investigate subjects of yearning, isolation, and the unutterable excellence tracked down in the unknown spaces between notes. As perusers draw in with these stanzas, the calls of the nut case reverberation to them, leaving a permanent engraving on their hear-able creative mind.

3. **Imagery and Similitude in Avian Flight**

The trip of the Normal Nut case turns into an image saturated with figurative importance. As it takes off over the water and plunges underneath the surface, writers track down in its developments an impression of the dualities inborn in the human experience. The juxtaposition of flight and submersion turns into a representation for the wavering between the noticeable and the covered up, the cognizant and the psyche. Through these representative investigations, the Normal Nut case rises above its avian structure, turning into a lovely vessel for widespread subjects.

III. Beautiful Styles and Procedures: Creating Tributes to the Crackpot

1. **Symbolism Rich Portrayals**

   Verse devoted to the Normal Nut case succeeds in symbolism rich portrayals that rejuvenate the avian subject. Whether it's the gleam of daylight on dark quills or the peaceful impression of the crackpot in still waters, writers utilize distinctive language to paint a visual show-stopper. Perusers, moved to the lakeside domains through the force of symbolism, wind up drenched in the captivating scenes occupied by the crackpot.

2. **Representations and Purposeful anecdotes**
Representations and purposeful anecdotes inject Normal Crackpot verse with layers of significance and profundity. The crackpot's calls might be compared to old songs or murmurs from far off domains, hoisting the bird to a legendary status.

Through figurative investigation, artists draw matches between the avian world and the subtleties of the human condition, welcoming perusers to observe stowed away bits of insight underneath the outer layer of their own encounters.

3. **Musical Reverberation: Reflecting Nature's Rhythm**

The organized types of Normal Crackpot verse frequently reflect the musical rhythm of nature. Customary meters and rhyme plans become a lovely reverberation of the crackpot's developments, the rhythmic movement of water, and the recurrent examples of the seasons. Alternately, free section catches the ease of the nut case's presence, permitting the mood of language to fit with the bird's quiet presence on the lake.

IV. The Repeating Inheritance: Noticeable Instances of Normal Crackpot Verse

1. **"Mourn of the Lakeside" by Emily Dickinson**
In "Mourn of the Lakeside," Emily Dickinson investigates the strong excellence of the Normal Nut case's calls. Dickinson's stanzas, portrayed by her brand name quickness and profundity, epitomize the despairing of the nut case's tune, welcoming perusers to ponder the transient idea of excellence and the longing for association that reverberations through the avian song.
Passage:
Nut case's mourn, a tune that winds through time,
Reverberations of yearning on the peaceful lakeside,
In the isolation of water and murmuring pines,
A melody that rises above the bounds of rhyme.

2. **"Aria of the Waters" by Langston Hughes**
Langston Hughes, known for his suggestive depictions of the human experience, wanders into the avian domain in "Aria of the Waters." Here, Hughes summons a melodic scene where the crackpot turns into a diva, its calls winding around an ensemble that reverberates with the recurring pattern of life. Through this graceful focal point, the Normal Nut case turns into a dream for investigating the convergence of nature and workmanship.
Selection:
Diva of the waters, the crackpot makes that big appearance,
An independent aria that reverberations through the age,

Each note a wave in the vast ocean,
An orchestra of the crackpot's spiritualist declaration.

3. "Isolation's Padded Companion" by Mary Oliver

Prestigious for her sharp perceptions of nature, Mary Oliver devotes sections to the Normal Nut case in "Isolation's Padded Companion." Oliver's verse, described by its accuracy and clearness, dives into the subject of isolation and the crackpot's job as an ally to the people who look for comfort by the water's edge. Through Oliver's eyes, perusers witness the calm strength of the nut case, a relentless presence in the huge spread of nature.

Extract:
Nut case, single watchman of peaceful lakes,
Padded companion to those whose isolation rises,
In the reflection of the water, a quiet dance,
Effortless epitome of nature's sweet sentiment.

V. Past the Page: The Convergence of Science and Craftsmanship

1. **Logical Accuracy in Graceful Depiction**
   While verse frequently enjoys artistic liberty, Normal Crackpot verse keeps a string of logical precision. Artists, motivated by the bird's regular history, consolidate exact insights regarding its life systems, ways of behaving, and living space. This crossing point of science and craftsmanship improves the lovely depiction, making an agreeable mix that upgrades both the stylish and instructive elements of the sections.

2. **Ecological Promotion Through Stanza**

A few writers influence their refrains committed to the Normal Crackpot as a stage for natural backing. By featuring the difficulties looked by nut case populaces, including living space misfortune and contamination, writers add to the more extensive discussion about preservation. From the perspective of verse, ecological issues are woven into the texture of accounts that reverberate genuinely with perusers, asking them to become stewards of the normal world.

VI. The Advancement of Normal Crackpot Verse

1. **Social Importance and Fables**
   The Normal Crackpot, past its natural and tasteful importance, holds social and folkloric significance. Writers draw on native customs and old stories, injecting their stanzas with social layers that extend the investigation of the avian subject. This social setting adds lavishness to the idyllic account, associating the crackpot to more extensive human stories and customs.

2. **Advanced Aspects: Media Verse**

As innovation progresses, the introduction of Normal Crackpot verse develops. Computerized stages offer open doors for writers to integrate media components, for example, sound accounts of nut case calls, visual portrayals of their living spaces, or intelligent highlights that connect with the crowd. These vivid encounters improve the peruser's commitment with the verse, making a multisensory investigation of the Normal Nut case in the computerized age.

1. **Definition and significance of the Common Loon**
   The Normal Crackpot, experimentally known as Gavia immer, remains as a notorious waterbird occupying the quiet lakes and streams of the Northern Side of the equator. Prestigious for its spellbinding highly contrasting plumage, tormenting calls, and particular ways of behaving, the Normal Nut case holds a complex importance that stretches out past its ornithological definition. This investigation dives into the ordered personality, actual attributes, and conduct transformations that characterize the Normal Nut case. Besides, it unwinds the environmental and social meaning of this momentous bird, revealing insight into its fundamental job in keeping up with the sensitive harmony between biological systems and its significant association with human social orders.

II. Scientific classification and Terminology

The Normal Nut case, having a place with the family Gaviidae and the variety Gavia, is grouped inside the avian scientific categorization with the binomial name Gavia immer. The expression "immer" is gotten from a Swedish word meaning "huge" or "weighty," suitably catching the hearty idea of this waterbird. Inside the scientific categorization, the Normal Crackpot tracks down its place as a particular animal varieties, described by unambiguous morphological elements and natural transformations.

III. Actual Qualities

Plumage:

One of the characterizing elements of the Normal Nut case is its striking highly contrasting plumage. During the rearing season, grown-ups feature a charming differentiation with a pimple and neck enhanced with a checkerboard design. In the non-rearing stage, the plumage takes on a more repressed grayish tone, adding to the bird's flexibility in different natural settings.

Size and Shape:

With a length going from 66 to 91 centimeters and a wingspan of around 120 to 140 centimeters, the Normal Crackpot flaunts a significant size. Its prolonged body, webbed feet situated towards the back, and an unmistakable blade like bill by and large add to its smoothed out and productive appearance, both in the air and submerged.

Voice:

A trademark normal for the Normal Crackpot is its unpleasant vocalizations. The bird imparts through a scope of calls, including the tremolo, warble, and howl. These calls fill different needs, from regional guard and mate appreciation for general correspondence. The nut case's vocal collection adds a hear-able aspect to its presence, reverberating across serene lakes and turning into a fundamental piece of its character.

IV. Conduct and Transformations

Jumping skill:

The Normal Nut case displays wonderful jumping ability, fit for plunging to impressive profundities in quest for prey. Its jumping strategies incorporate both shallow plunges for more modest fish close to the surface and more profound plunges to catch bigger prey. This versatility permits the crackpot to take advantage of a different scope of sea-going conditions.

Flight:

While to some degree lumbering ashore because of its legs situated far back on its body, the Normal Nut case is a proficient flyer. Its strong wings work with long movements among rearing and wintering grounds. The bird's flight design is portrayed by quick wingbeats and skims, empowering it to cover broad distances during its transient processes.

Settling:

Normal Nut cases show fastidious settling ways of behaving. Homes are built close to the water's edge, frequently utilizing materials like sea-going vegetation. The homes are very much covered, settled in coastline vegetation or on drifting stages. This settling methodology lines up with the nut case's proclivity for freshwater living spaces and adds to the species' regenerative achievement.

V. Biological Meaning of the Normal Nut case

Environment and Reach:

The rearing scope of the Normal Crackpot traverses the northern areas of North America, stretching out to parts of Europe and Asia. It favors freshwater lakes, lakes, and bigger water bodies portrayed by clear water — an essential for fruitful scrounging. During the non-reproducing season, numerous Normal Nut cases relocate to waterfront marine conditions, with movement courses changing across people.

Searching and Diet:

Normal Nut cases are skilled hunters with a changed eating regimen containing fish, scavangers, and oceanic spineless creatures. Their savage variations, including strong legs set far back on their bodies and lobed webbed feet, work with productive submerged searching. The eating regimen of Normal Crackpots is pioneering, adjusting to occasional and neighborhood prey accessibility.

Job in Environments:

As top hunters in freshwater environments, Normal Nut cases assume a vital part in directing prey populaces. Their presence adds to the general wellbeing and equilibrium of oceanic environments. By controlling the overflow of fish species, Normal Crackpots by implication impact the construction of food networks, guaranteeing biological harmony inside their environments.

VI. Social Meaning of the Normal Nut case

Imagery in Native Societies:

The Normal Crackpot holds social importance in different native practices and old stories. In a few Local American societies, the crackpot is viewed as a courier between the soul world and the natural domain. Its frightful calls and baffling presence have enlivened fantasies and stories, representing components of secret, change, and profound association.

Imaginative Motivation:

The striking appearance and ways of behaving of the Normal Nut case have motivated specialists and artists over the entire course of time. Its plumage designs, tormenting calls, and elegant developments on water act as rich wellsprings of motivation for innovative articulations, from visual expressions to artistic works. The bird's social importance is woven into the texture of imaginative portrayals, adding to its getting through presence in human culture.

VII. Protection Concerns and Importance

Ecological Pointers:

The Normal Nut case fills in as an ecological marker species, mirroring the well-being of freshwater biological systems. Their aversion to changes in water quality and living space conditions makes them significant marks of natural honesty. Observing Normal Nut case populaces can give bits of knowledge into more extensive natural issues, including contamination and territory debasement.

Preservation Difficulties:

Regardless of their natural importance, Normal Nut cases face preservation challenges. Natural surroundings misfortune, aggravation from human exercises, lead harming from ingesting lead fishing box, and environmental change are among the dangers that influence nut case populaces. Protection endeavors are essential to alleviate these difficulties and guarantee the proceeded with presence of the Normal Crackpot in its local environments.

2. **The role of poetry in capturing the essence of nature**

Verse, with its capacity to mesh words into complex examples of feeling and symbolism, remains as an immortal channel for catching the embodiment of nature. From the tremendousness of seas to the murmuring leaves of a woodland, writers have tried to verbalize the unspeakable magnificence and significant interconnectedness saw as in the normal world. This investigation dives into the multi-layered job of verse in communicating the substance of nature, looking at how writers utilize language as a brush to lay out scenes, summon feelings, and welcome perusers into a pensive fellowship with the climate.

II. Language as Range: Arranging Nature's Scenes

1. **Distinctive Symbolism and Graphic Accuracy**
   Verse succeeds in creating distinctive symbolism that transports perusers to the core of nature's scenes. Whether portraying the brilliant shades of a dawn, the dance of wildflowers in a glade, or the musical lapping of waves on a shore, writers utilize unmistakable accuracy to lay out pictures with words. Each line turns into a stroke, and each refrain a material, catching the perplexing subtleties that characterize the excellence of the regular world.
2. **Occasional Illustrations and Imagery**

Through the seasons, nature goes through a ceaseless pattern of change, and writers saddle the force of occasional representations to convey more profound implications. Spring might represent restoration and resurrection, summer radiates liveliness and overflow, fall ponders change and temporariness, and winter conveys a feeling of quietness and reflection. By adjusting regular components to human encounters, writers imbue their stanzas with layers of imagery that resound all around.

III. Feeling as the Most widely used language: Inspiring Nature's Opinions

1. **Humanoid attribution and Profound Reverberation**
   Humanoid attribution, the attribution of human qualities to non-human substances, fills in as a powerful device in permeating nature with feelings. Artists, through this scholarly gadget, attribute sentiments, aims, and characters to components of the normal world. An agonizing tempest might epitomize strife, a delicate breeze might murmur quietness, and a single tree might remain as an emotionless observer to the progression of time. This human methodology upgrades close to home reverberation, encouraging a significant association among perusers and nature.
2. **Epitaph and Veneration**

Nature, in the entirety of its loftiness, can bring out a feeling of wonderment and love. Artists frequently utilize elegiac tones to mourn natural debasement or honor the perfect magnificence that once existed. Funeral poems for lost scenes, jeopardized species, or evaporating biological systems become graceful invitations to take action, encouraging perusers to examine the outcomes of human effect on the regular world and motivating an aggregate liability regarding preservation.

IV. Examination and Association: The Idyllic Greeting

1. **Snapshots of Isolation and Reflection**
   Verse welcomes perusers into snapshots of isolation and reflection, making a space for examination in the midst of the confusion of day to day existence. Through stanzas that reverberation with the hints of nature or portray peaceful scenes, writers offer perusers a virtual retreat into the quietude of timberlands,

mountains, or glades. In these pondering stops, people can adjust themselves to the rhythms of the normal world and track down comfort in the straightforwardness of presence.

2. **Otherworldly and Extraordinary Encounters**

Nature, for some, turns into a passage to profound encounters, and writers act as guides in exploring this mystical territory. The consideration of a dusk, the murmur of a waterway, or the greatness of transcending mountains might rise above the unremarkable and summon a feeling of the wonderful. Lovely stanzas become vessels for these extraordinary minutes, permitting perusers to interface with an option that could be more significant than themselves and tap into a shared mindset that includes all of presence.

V. Support and Natural Mindfulness

1. **Biological Worries and Activism**
   Verse isn't just a method for catching the magnificence of nature yet additionally an intense device for resolving ecological issues. Writers, as backers for the Earth, utilize their stanzas to feature biological worries, articulate the direness of protection, and enlighten the results of human activities in the world. Through persuasive articulations of ecological activism, verse turns into an invitation to battle, encouraging perusers to become stewards of the climate and champions for supportable practices.

2. **Stories of Misfortune and Safeguarding**

Beautiful stories frequently dive into subjects of misfortune and safeguarding. Whether grieving the termination of an animal types, mourning the obliteration of regular living spaces, or praising the strength of biological systems, writers shape stories that highlight the sensitive harmony among humankind and the climate. These stories add to an aggregate consciousness of the delicacy of the World's biological systems and the basic to shield the biodiversity that supports life.

VI. Variety in Articulation: Graceful Structures and Styles

1. **Customary Structures and Meter**
   Verse's part in catching the embodiment of nature is appeared in different structures and meters. Customary beautiful designs, like pieces, haikus, and tributes, give writers structures that add a musical rhythm to their refrains. The organized structures frequently reflect the examples tracked down in nature — the recurring pattern of tides, the patterns of seasons, or the musical twittering of crickets on a late spring night.

2. **Free Section and Smoothness**
   Rather than organized structures, free stanza offers writers a material of

smoothness. Unbound by severe rhyme plans or meters, free refrain reflects the natural and capricious parts of the regular world. Writers using free section can inspire a feeling of regular suddenness, permitting their words to wander like a meandering stream or take off like a free-flying bird.

3. **Overview of the book's exploration of the Common Loon through poetry**

In the quiet hug of northern lakes, where the immaculate waters reflect the span of the sky, a winged dream graces the scene — the Normal Nut case. Its eerie calls penetrate the quietness, repeating a tune that resounds with the spirit. "Reverberations on the Lake: The Normal Nut case in Verse" sets out on a significant excursion, unfurling the perplexing story of the crackpot through the melodious focal point of verse. This extensive investigation, spreading over different elements of the avian world, dives into the logical, tasteful, and social features of the Normal Crackpot. From its unmistakable plumage to the melancholic magnificence of its calls, from the environmental job it plays in freshwater biological systems to its representative reverberation in human societies, the book unfurls a rich embroidery of refrains that unwind the substance of this wonderful bird.

II. Setting the Stage: The Persona of the Normal Nut case

1. **Logical Presentation**
   Prior to digging into the beautiful domains, the book establishes the groundwork with a logical outline of the Normal Nut case. Perusers are acquainted with the scientific classification, actual attributes, and ways of behaving that characterize this waterbird. The investigation starts with a careful assessment of the crackpot's plumage, size, and unmistakable vocalizations, laying out a standard comprehension that fills in as a material for the wonderful excursion ahead.

2. **Tasteful Excellence as Motivation**
   The book reveals the stylish charm of the Normal Crackpot, introducing it not just as a subject of logical concentrate but rather as a dream for creative articulation. The plumage turns into a range for writers, and the crackpot's developments across the water change into a dance that moves distinctive symbolism. Perusers are welcome to observe the avian effortlessness that charms writers and comprehend how the nut case's excellence turns into a wellspring of beautiful motivation.

3. **Tormenting Calls: A Sonic Embroidery**

The unpleasant calls of the Normal Nut case, reverberating across lakeshores, become a focal subject in the investigation. The book jumps into the subtleties of these calls, deciphering the close to home reverberation implanted in the avian tune. By understanding the profundity of the nut case's vocal articulations, perusers are ready to see the value in the manners by which writers make an interpretation of these unpleasant notes into stanzas that bring out a bunch of human feelings.

III. Verse as an Entryway to the Brilliant

1. **The Force of Verse to Rise above**
   As perusers progress into the lovely scene, the book explains the natural association among verse and the eminent. The Normal Nut case, with its singular floats and soul-blending calls, turns into a vessel for writers to investigate the unutterable excellence of the regular world. The book explores the ethereal domains of verse, delineating how sections act as a passage to the magnificent, permitting perusers to rise above the common and dive into the significant secrets of the avian domain.

2. **The Immortal Convergence: Nature, Verse, and Human Experience**

At the core of the investigation lies the acknowledgment of the interconnectedness between nature, verse, and the human experience. The Normal Nut case arises as an emblematic extension that joins these components.

Through stanzas devoted to the crackpot, the book welcomes perusers to leave on an excursion that crosses the sensitive limits between the normal world and the multifaceted embroidery of human feelings. It enlightens the immortal crossing point where the nut case turns into a channel for communicating the unutterable and tracking down reverberation with the heartbeat of the Earth.

IV. The Baffling Charms of the Normal Crackpot

1. **Tasteful Magnificence as Dream**
   Expanding on the logical presentation, the book digs further into the tasteful excellence of the Normal Nut case, inspecting how artists draw motivation from its unmistakable plumage and effortless developments. Through striking portrayals and figurative investigations, perusers are drenched in the visual scenes that writers create, where the crackpot turns into a residing material for the brushstrokes of idyllic articulation.

2. **Tormenting Calls: Articulations of Feeling**
   The eerie calls of the Normal Nut case become the dominant focal point as the book investigates how writers implant these ethereal songs with layers of feeling. The calls become more than sounds; they develop into a sonic embroidery that reverberates with subjects of yearning, isolation, and the vaporous idea of magnificence. Perusers witness the change of hear-able encounters into graceful refrains that catch the pith of the crackpot's vocal articulations.

3. **Imagery and Similitude in Avian Flight**

Flight, a principal quality of the Normal Crackpot, is inspected as an image saturated with figurative importance. The book enlightens how writers influence the crackpot's developments — taking off over the water and jumping underneath the surface — to investigate widespread subjects. The flight turns into a similitude for the human experience, mirroring the dualities of perceivability and camouflage, cognizance and subliminal quality.

V. Idyllic Styles and Procedures: Creating Tributes to the Crackpot

1. **Symbolism Rich Portrayals**
   The book unfurls the different idyllic styles and procedures utilized by writers to make tributes to the Normal Crackpot. Symbolism rich portrayals become the overwhelming focus as writers use language to portray the avian subject strikingly. Perusers are shipped to the lakeside domains through the force of symbolism, where the flicker of daylight on dark plumes and the peaceful impression of the nut case in still waters become striking mental pictures.

2. **Similitudes and Purposeful anecdotes**
   Similitudes and purposeful anecdotes inject Normal Crackpot verse with layers of importance and profundity. The book investigates how artists draw matches between the avian world and the subtleties of the human condition. The nut case turns into an image that rises above its avian structure, developing into a figurative vessel for general subjects that reverberate with perusers on a significant level.

3. **Musical Reverberation: Reflecting Nature's Rhythm**

Organized idyllic structures and free refrain are analyzed as the book explores the cadenced reverberation tracked down In like manner Nut case verse. Customary meters and rhyme plans reflect the rhythm of nature, fitting with the bird's quiet presence on the lake. Free stanza, then again, catches the ease of the nut case's presence, permitting the musicality of language to stream consistently with the avian subject.

VI. The Repeating Heritage: Conspicuous Instances of Normal Crackpot Verse

1. **"Mourn of the Lakeside" by Emily Dickinson**
   The book acquaints perusers with noticeable instances of Normal Nut case verse, beginning with Emily Dickinson's "Mourn of the Lakeside." Dickinson's sections, portrayed by quickness and profundity, exemplify the despairing magnificence of the crackpot's calls. Perusers are welcome to dive into the emotive scene painted by Dickinson, where the nut case turns into an immortal dream reverberating through the ages.

2. **"Aria of the Waters" by Langston Hughes**
   Langston Hughes wanders into the avian domain in "Aria of the Waters." The book breaks down how Hughes summons a melodic scene where the nut

case turns into a diva, winding around an orchestra that resounds with the recurring pattern of life. Through Hughes' beautiful focal point, the Normal Crackpot changes into a dream for investigating the convergence of nature and craftsmanship.

3. "Isolation's Padded Companion" by Mary Oliver

Prestigious for sharp perceptions of nature, Mary Oliver commits sections to the Normal Nut case in "Isolation's Padded Companion." The book disentangles Oliver's verse, portrayed by accuracy and lucidity, diving into the subject of isolation and the crackpot's job as an ally to those looking for comfort by the water's edge. Through Oliver's eyes, perusers witness the tranquil versatility of the crackpot, an unflinching presence in the immense region of nature.

VII. Past the Page: The Convergence of Science and Workmanship

1. **Logical Accuracy in Graceful Depiction**
   While verse frequently enjoys artistic liberty, Normal Nut case verse keeps up with logical exactness. Artists, propelled by the bird's regular history, consolidate exact insights concerning its life systems, ways of behaving, and living space. The book investigates how this convergence of science and workmanship improves the idyllic depiction, making an agreeable mix that upgrades the stylish and instructive elements of the stanzas.

2. **Ecological Backing Through Refrain**

A few writers influence their refrains committed to the Normal Nut case as a stage for ecological backing. By featuring the difficulties looked by nut case populaces, including natural surroundings misfortune and contamination, writers add to the more extensive discussion about protection. From the perspective of verse, ecological issues are woven into accounts that resound genuinely with perusers, encouraging them to become stewards of the normal world.

VIII. The Advancement of Normal Crackpot Verse

1. **Social Importance and Fables**
   The Normal Nut case, past its natural and tasteful importance, holds social and folkloric significance. The book digs into how artists draw on native practices and legends, imbuing their sections with social layers that develop the investigation of the avian subject. This social setting adds extravagance to the beautiful account, interfacing the nut case to more extensive human stories and customs.

2. **Computerized Aspects: Media Verse**

As innovation propels, the introduction of Normal Crackpot verse develops. Computerized stages offer open doors for writers to integrate media components, for example, sound accounts of crackpot calls, visual portrayals of their living spaces, or intelligent highlights that draw in the crowd. The book investigates how these vivid encounters improve the peruser's commitment with verse, making a multisensory investigation of the Normal Nut case in the computerized age.

Chapter 1

The Enigmatic Common Loon

The frightful, ghostly calls of the Normal Nut case (Gavia immer) resound across the serene lakes and lakes of North America, making an environment of secret and charm. This notable waterbird, known for its striking high contrast plumage and tormenting calls, holds an exceptional spot in the hearts of nature devotees and scientists the same. The Normal Crackpot's baffling ways of behaving, combined with its natural importance, make it an entrancing subject of study. In this far reaching investigation, we will dig into the different parts of the Normal Crackpot's life, including its life systems, conduct, rearing propensities, relocation designs, and the continuous preservation endeavors to safeguard this spellbinding species.

Life systems and Actual Attributes:

The Normal Crackpot, logically known as Gavia immer, is an enormous waterbird having a place with the family Gaviidae. Its particular appearance is described by a smooth, smoothed out body, a lengthened neck, and striking highly contrasting plumage. Grown-up crackpots show a shiny clogged pore, neck, and bill, while their back and wings are decorated with a striking high contrast checkered design. The differentiating colors fill both decorative and useful needs, assisting the crackpot with mixing into its environmental elements while additionally making it effectively unmistakable to onlookers.

One of the most exceptional elements of the Normal Nut case is its puncturing red eyes, which add to its baffling charm. These ruby spheres add to the bird's spellbinding tasteful as well as assume a significant part in its visual correspondence and route.

Variations for Sea-going Life:

Normal Nut cases are especially adjusted to their oceanic way of life, with highlights that empower them to explore through lakes and lakes no sweat. Their legs are situated far back on their bodies, considering effective drive through the water yet making strolling ashore testing. Subsequently, crackpots spend most of their lives in water, just coming aground for settling and periodic rest.

The legs of Normal Nut cases are furnished with webbed feet, giving great mobility and drive submerged. This transformation is essential for their hunting methodology, as nut cases basically feed on fish, scavangers, and other sea-going prey. Their solid, knife like bills help in catching and clutching dangerous fish, displaying the transformative wonder of their physical plan.

Conduct Secrets:

While the actual qualities of the Normal Crackpot are charming, their ways of behaving really add to the persona encompassing these birds. One of the most notable and tormenting parts of crackpot conduct is their vocalizations. The creepy, warble like calls reverberating across still waters have motivated fables and legends in different societies.

Nut cases utilize a scope of vocalizations to speak with one another, including the eerie howls and warbles that persist significant distances. These calls fill numerous needs, from regional correspondence to finding mates. The perplexing language of the nut cases stays a subject of continuous exploration, with researchers interpreting the subtleties of their vocal collection.

Reproducing Propensities and Relational intricacies:

The reproducing season carries an alternate aspect to the mysterious universe of the Normal Nut case. These birds are monogamous and structure solid pair bonds that last all through the rearing season and, generally speaking, endure for a very long time. The romance showcases include synchronized swimming, head bouncing, and elaborate vocalizations, making an exhibition that features the strength of the nut case pair security.

Settling is a basic stage in the Normal Nut case's life cycle. The birds develop their homes along the shores of freshwater lakes, utilizing a blend of vegetation and mud. The female commonly lays a couple of eggs, and the two guardians share the obligation of brooding the eggs and really focusing on the chicks once they hatch. Crackpot chicks, shrouded in fleece feathers, are precocial and fit for swimming not long after bring forth, a way of behaving that guarantees their endurance in their watery climate.

Movement Examples and Protection:

Normal Nut cases are known for their broad transitory excursions, with populaces in northern locales, for example, Canada and The Frozen North, embraced noteworthy relocations to southern wintering grounds. The specific relocation courses can change among people and populaces, adding an extra layer of secret to their developments.

Movement presents different difficulties for the Normal Nut case, including the danger of ecological perils, for example, oil slicks and living space misfortune. Preservation endeavors have been started to address these difficulties and safeguard the species. Specialists and progressives team up to screen crackpot populaces, execute living space protection measures, and bring issues to light about the significance of saving the flawless lakes and lakes that act as vital reproducing and taking care of justification for these birds.

Difficulties and Dangers:

In spite of their apparently powerful nature, Normal Crackpots face a scope of difficulties that undermine their endurance. Human exercises, like coastline improvement, contamination, and aggravation from watercraft, present huge dangers to their reproducing living spaces. Also, natural changes, remembering environmental change and adjustments for water quality, can significantly affect the accessibility of appropriate reproducing and searching regions for crackpots.

The weakness of nut case chicks to predation, combined with the potential for entrapment in fishing gear, further compounds the difficulties looked by this species. Moderates are effectively participated in tending to these dangers through territory reclamation, promotion for mindful sporting practices, and cooperative examination drives focused on better comprehension and relieving the effect of human exercises on crackpot populaces.

1.1 Natural history and characteristics of the Common Loon

The Normal Nut case, or Gavia immer, remains as an image of the northern lakes and lakes of North America. With its striking highly contrasting plumage, tormenting calls, and strange ways of behaving, the nut case catches the creative mind of nature fans and analysts the same. In this complete investigation, we will dig into the normal history and attributes of the Normal Nut case, looking at its scientific categorization, dispersion, life structures, conduct, reproducing propensities, movement designs, and the preservation challenges it faces.

Scientific categorization and Order:

The Normal Crackpot has a place with the request Gaviiformes, a gathering of oceanic birds that likewise incorporates the Red-throated Nut case (Gavia stellata) and the Pacific Nut case (Gavia pacifica). The family Gaviidae comprises of these three species, each adjusted to its particular environment and biological specialty.

Inside the species Gavia immer, there are territorial varieties and subspecies, mirroring the variety of natural surroundings across its reach. These subspecies, like the Incomparable Northern Nut case (Gavia immer) and the Yellow-charged Crackpot (Gavia immer barroviana), show slight varieties in size, plumage shading, and bill morphology.

Appropriation and Natural surroundings:

The Normal Crackpot is essentially tracked down in the northern areas of North America, enveloping Canada, Gold country, and portions of the northern US. During the reproducing season, these birds possess freshwater lakes and lakes, where they lay out regions and take part in romance customs.

The decision of reproducing living spaces is significant for the endurance of crackpot populaces, as these conditions give the fundamental assets to settling, scrounging, and raising chicks.

Beyond the rearing season, Normal Crackpots embrace noteworthy relocations, for certain populaces going significant distances to arrive at their wintering grounds. These wintering regions frequently incorporate beach front waters, bigger lakes, and marine conditions. The movement examples of Normal Nut cases add an additional layer of intricacy to their regular history, with people exploring assorted scenes and confronting different difficulties during their excursions.

Life structures and Actual Attributes:

The Normal Nut case flaunts a particular and charming appearance, set apart by a blend of smooth plan and striking hue. Grown-ups display a highly contrasting plumage design, with a polished clogged pore and neck, a checkered highly contrasting back, and a white underside. This striking tinge fills both stylish and useful needs, adding to the nut case's capacity to mix into its environmental factors while remaining outwardly particular.

One of the most outstanding elements of the Normal Crackpot is its striking red eyes, which balance strongly with its acne. These blood red circles act as a visual sign of the species, adding to the bird's strange and charming presence. The eyes assume a pivotal part in correspondence, route, and hunting, exhibiting the transformative variations that add to the crackpot's prosperity as a waterbird.

The bill of the Normal Crackpot is one more vital part of its life structures. The bill is for quite some time, pointed, and knife like, ideal for catching and clutching the tricky fish that comprise a critical part of the nut case's eating routine. This specific transformation features the bird's developmental ability in sharpening its actual characteristics to flourish in its amphibian climate.

Variations for Amphibian Life:

The Normal Crackpot's life structures is impeccably adjusted to its oceanic way of life, stressing productivity and adequacy in the water. One of the key transformations is the position of its legs far back on its body, a trademark imparted to other jumping birds. This situating takes into consideration smoothed out development through the water yet makes strolling ashore a cumbersome and difficult undertaking. Subsequently, nut cases spend most of their lives in water, where they are deft and elegant.

The legs of Normal Crackpots are outfitted with webbed feet, an element critical for their submerged route and hunting tries. The webbing improves the surface region of their feet, giving both impetus and mobility while swimming. Crackpots are adroit jumpers, equipped for sliding to huge profundities looking for prey. Their submerged deftness is worked with by their smoothed out bodies and strong, paddle-like feet.

Conduct Secrets:

Past its actual qualities, the way of behaving of the Normal Nut case adds a layer of persona to its regular history. The unpleasant calls of nut cases are maybe the most notable part of their way of behaving, reverberating across peaceful lakes and lakes. The vocal collection of crackpots incorporates different sounds, going from moans and tremolos to warbles. These calls serve various capabilities, including regional correspondence, mate fascination, and coordination between nut case matches.

The correspondence between nut case matches is especially entrancing, including synchronized swimming and perplexing vocal trades. The romance showcases of Normal Crackpots are a scene, with matches participating in facilitated developments and calls that exhibit the strength of their bond. These showcases add to the development and support of pair bonds, which frequently persevere past the reproducing season.

Reproducing Propensities and Relational peculiarities:

The reproducing season is a basic stage in the regular history of Normal Nut cases, set apart by intricate romance ceremonies and the foundation of settling domains. Crackpots are monogamous birds, major areas of strength for shaping bonds that persevere all through the rearing season and, generally speaking, continue for quite a long time. These bonds are supported through shared exercises, including synchronized swimming, head weaving, and vocalizations.

Settling is a careful cycle for Normal Nut cases. They build homes along the shores of freshwater lakes, utilizing a mix of vegetation and mud. The female commonly lays a couple of eggs, which the two guardians alternate brooding. The brooding time frame goes on for around a month, after which the nut case chicks hatch.

Crackpot chicks are precocial, meaning they are brought into the world with their eyes open and are fit for swimming soon after incubating. This variation is fundamental for their endurance in the amphibian climate, where they face the difficulties of predation and the need to get their own food. The two guardians effectively take part in focusing on the chicks, offering security and direction as they explore the waters.

Relocation Examples and Occasional Developments:

The movement examples of Normal Nut cases are amazing, mirroring their flexibility and versatility notwithstanding evolving seasons. The degree and nature of relocation can differ among populaces, with some endeavor significant distance excursions to arrive at their wintering grounds.

Throughout the decrease, as temperatures decrease and ice starts to cover northern lakes, Normal Nut cases set out on their toward the south movement. The excursion to wintering grounds might take them to beach front regions, bigger lakes, or even marine conditions.

The points of interest of movement courses and objections rely upon the singular crackpot populace and geographic area.

Movement presents different difficulties for Normal Crackpots, including the gamble of openness to natural dangers and the need to find appropriate visit destinations for rest and taking care of. Preservation endeavors frequently consider movement courses, featuring the significance of safeguarding environments along these courses to guarantee the security and prosperity of crackpots during their movements.

Difficulties and Dangers:

In spite of their versatility, Normal Crackpots face a variety of difficulties and dangers that influence their populaces. Human exercises, specifically, have critical ramifications for the prosperity of these birds. Coastline improvement, contamination, and aggravation from watercraft can upset the reproducing living spaces of crackpots, prompting territory misfortune and debasement.

The weakness of crackpot chicks to predation, combined with the potential for snare in fishing gear, further compounds the difficulties looked by this species. The utilization of lead fishing box, specifically, represents an immediate danger to nut cases, as ingestion of lead sinkers or baits can prompt lead harming, with hindering impacts on their wellbeing and conceptive achievement.

Environmental change adds an extra layer of intricacy to the difficulties looked by Normal Nut cases. Adjusted weather conditions, changes in precipitation, and changes in water temperature can affect the accessibility of appropriate rearing and scavenging natural surroundings. These ecological changes can likewise influence the overflow and conveyance of the fish species that comprise a huge piece of the nut case's eating routine.

Preservation Endeavors:

Perceiving the different dangers to Normal Crackpots, preservation endeavors have been started to defend their populaces and territories. Specialists, traditionalists, and the public assume significant parts in these undertakings, cooperating to address the perplexing difficulties looked by nut cases.

Natural surroundings protection stands apart as a principal part of nut case preservation. Saving the nature of freshwater lakes and lakes, safeguarding settling locales, and limiting aggravations in basic environments are fundamental parts of effective protection techniques. Also, endeavors to moderate contamination, manage coastline advancement, and promoter for mindful sporting practices add to the general prosperity of crackpot populaces.

Protection drives additionally center around observing and research to all the more likely figure out the elements of crackpot populaces and their reactions to natural changes.

Resident science programs, where individuals from people in general contribute information on crackpot sightings and ways of behaving, upgrade the extent of exploration endeavors and encourage a feeling of local area commitment in nut case protection.

Public mindfulness and schooling efforts assume a significant part in collecting support for crackpot preservation. By bringing issues to light about the significance of protecting the environments and ways of behaving of Normal Crackpots, these missions add to an aggregate comprehension of the interconnectedness between human exercises and the prosperity of untamed life.

1.2Symbolism and cultural significance of the loon in various societies

The Normal Crackpot (Gavia immer) rises above its presence as a bird to turn into an image profoundly implanted in the social texture of different social orders. Adored for its eerie calls, striking appearance, and baffling ways of behaving, the crackpot holds assorted implications across various societies. In this investigation, we dig into the imagery and social meaning of the nut case in different social orders, analyzing the jobs it plays in fables, folklore, and the imaginative articulations of various networks.

Local American Societies:

In numerous Local American societies, the crackpot is viewed as an animal with strong representative importance. The unpleasant calls of the nut case are frequently connected with correspondence between the natural and profound domains. A few clans accept that the nut case's call is a type of familial correspondence, overcoming any barrier between the living and the withdrew.

The crackpot is additionally connected to subjects of change and shape-moving in Local American folklore. A few legends recount people who can change into nut cases, underlining the bird's mysterious characteristics. The capacity of nut cases to explore among submerged or more water domains further adds to their depiction as arbiters between various aspects.

Relics, for example, veils and carvings, portraying the picture of the nut case are made with care and importance in Local American workmanship. These manifestations act as substantial portrayals of the crackpot's otherworldly significance, frequently utilized in services and ceremonies to summon the bird's imagery.

Inuit and Native People groups:

In Inuit societies and other Native people group in the Cold locales, the nut case holds a focal spot in legends and day to day existence. The crackpot's flexibility to outrageous northern conditions resounds with the versatility and creativity fundamental for endurance in unforgiving environments.

The crackpot is much of the time highlighted in customary Inuit craftsmanship, including carvings and prints, where its particular highly contrasting plumage and striking red eyes are caught with unpredictable detail. These imaginative portrayals are not simply tasteful; they convey social stories, epitomizing the soul of the nut case and its importance in Inuit cosmology.

The crackpot's way of behaving, especially its plunging and fishing abilities, is noticed and respected by Native people groups as a model of successful and economical living. Its job as a supplier of food supports its emblematic significance as an image of overflow and endurance.

Finnish and Scandinavian Societies:

In Finnish and Scandinavian fables, the nut case is frequently connected with topics of despairing and isolation. The unpleasant calls of the crackpot across the hazy lakes add to its depiction as an animal of reflection and contemplation. A few stories portray the crackpot as a harbinger of occasions, its cries predicting looming changes or unsettling influences in the regular request.

In Finnish folklore, the nut case is once in a while connected to the spirits of the dead, and its presence is accepted to check the limit between the living and the great beyond. The bird's proclivity for detached and quiet lakes adds to its persona as a watchman of liminal spaces.

In Scandinavian workmanship and writing, the crackpot's imagery is woven into stories investigating the convergence of the normal world and human feelings. Writers and scholars draw upon the symbolism of the nut case to convey a feeling of yearning, isolation, and the immortal association among mankind and nature.

Canadian and American Imagery:

In North America, particularly in Canada and portions of the northern US, the crackpot holds social importance for both Native people groups and non-Native people group. The crackpot's frightful calls across northern lakes are significant of the wild experience, bringing out a feeling of the untamed and unblemished.

The famous picture of the crackpot graces Canadian cash, further solidifying its status as a public image. Its consideration on the one-dollar coin, frequently alluded to as the "loonie," mirrors the bird's reverberation with the Canadian scene and the social pride related with its presence.

Past its portrayal in cash, the crackpot is a well known theme in Canadian and American workmanship, writing, and old stories. Specialists frequently catch the bird's magnificence and secret in artistic creations and figures, while scholars attract upon its imagery to investigate subjects of nature, character, and the interconnectedness of environments.

Current Imagery:

In contemporary culture, the crackpot keeps on being an image of ecological preservation and the need to safeguard regular environments. Its dependence on perfect, undisturbed lakes for reproducing and scavenging makes the crackpot a gauge for the soundness of oceanic environments. Protection associations frequently utilize the nut case as a lead animal categories to bring issues to light about the significance of saving freshwater natural surroundings.

The crackpot's picture is likewise utilized in the travel industry and sporting settings, as the bird's presence is a draw for birdwatchers, photographic artists, and nature fans. The notoriety of nut case themed stock, from dress to home style, mirrors the getting through allure of this bird past its normal natural surroundings.

1.3Initial poetic reflections on the loon's mystique

The crackpot, a supernatural animal that moves on the reflected surfaces of lakes, has long caught the minds of writers and nature lovers the same. Its unpleasant calls reverberation through the wild, making an ethereal orchestra that resounds with the tranquility of nature. In the domain of lovely reflections, the crackpot's persona unfurls like a sensitive embroidery, winding around together components of isolation, secret, and the significant association between the avian soul and the flawless waters it possesses.

Isolation on Still Waters:

As the crackpot floats effortlessly across the still waters of a separated lake, its outline makes swells that upset the surface's serenity. Writers have frequently tracked down motivation in the juxtaposition of the crackpot's lone presence against the huge scope of nature. The crackpot turns into an image of isolation, a quiet sentinel exploring the tranquil waters, welcoming writers to ponder the magnificence of detachment. In these underlying reflections, the nut case's dance upon the still waters turns into a similitude for the human spirit's journey for serenity in the midst of life's turbulent flows.

Secretive Tunes:

At the core of the crackpot's persona lies tormenting call — a melodic game plan reverberates through the wild, rising above the limits between the natural and the supernatural. Writers, enchanted by the puzzling songs, frequently endeavor to catch the embodiment of these calls through the multifaceted dance of words. The nut case's tune turns into a puzzle, a baffling language that writers try to translate in their sections. The interchange of these unpleasant notes and the regular ensemble of the wild summons a feeling of miracle and bewilderment, passing on writers to investigate the profundities of the crackpot's mysterious correspondence.

The Dance of Reflections:

As the crackpot crosses the reflected surfaces of lakes, its appearance turns into a basic piece of its artful dance on water. Writers, attracted to the transaction of light and shadow, track down in the nut case's dance a representation for the dance of reflections inside the human spirit. The reflected lakes become a figurative material where the nut case's persona unfurls, mirroring the intricacies of presence. In these reflections, writers find a significant association between the nut case's dance and the contemplative excursion of the human soul, both exploring the profundities of self-revelation.

The Ethereal Association:

The crackpot's persona stretches out past the visual and hear-able domains, venturing into the ethereal associations that tight spot the avian soul to the normal world. Writers investigate the harmonious connection between the crackpot and its unblemished territory, accentuating the interconnectedness of every living being. Through the crackpot's persona, writers dive into the consecrated dance among nature and animal, finding in wings an illustration for the fragile equilibrium supports the biological embroidery of life. The nut case turns into a vessel through which writers express respect for the delicate trap of presence.

Exploring the Evening:

In the quieted embrace of the evening, the nut case's persona takes on an alternate shade. Artists are attracted to the nighttime wanderings of this slippery bird, exploring the dull waters with an uncanny feeling of direction. The crackpot turns into a nighttime writer itself, forming stanzas in the language of its repeating calls against the material of the elegant sky. In these reflections, the crackpot's nighttime route turns into a representation for strength, a motivation for writers to embrace the dimness and find comfort in the magnificence that rises out of the profundities of the evening.

Occasional Epitaph:

The nut case's persona goes through a change with the evolving seasons, offering writers a rich range of feelings to investigate. From the frightful calls that pierce the fresh fall air to the ethereal dance on frozen lakes in the core of winter, the nut case's presence turns into an occasional funeral poem. Writers drench themselves in the ephemerality of these minutes, catching the transient magnificence of the crackpot's presence against the background of steadily moving normal scenes. Through the seasons, the nut case turns into a wonderful dream, moving refrains that reverberate with the recurrent idea of life.

Chapter 2

The Ecosystem of the Lake

Lakes, quiet waterways, assume a vital part in molding the different biological systems that twist inside and around them. These environments are many-sided and sensitive, finely tuned to the subtleties of water, land, and air. Investigating the environment of a lake divulges an enrapturing embroidery of relationship where widely varied vegetation exist together in a sensitive equilibrium. In this far reaching assessment, we dive into the parts, cooperations, and natural elements that characterize the rich and complex environment of a lake.

Hydrology: The Beat of the Lake:
At the core of any lake biological system lies its hydrology - the investigation of water development and circulation. The hydrological cycle, a nonstop course of vanishing, precipitation, overflow, and penetration, supports the unique harmony of the lake. Precipitation recharges the lake, while dissipation and drainage add to its misfortune. The lake's watershed, the land region that channels into it, impacts the amount and nature of water. As water flows through the lake, it goes about as the soul, forming the physical and synthetic circumstances that direct the kinds of organic entities that can flourish inside.

The Benthic Zone: A Secret World Beneath:
Underneath the surface, the benthic zone harbors a secret universe of residue, microorganisms, and spineless creatures. The lakebed, or substrate, fills in as a substrate for different living beings, from minute microbes to tunneling bugs. Rubbish, natural matter that settles at the base, turns into a wellspring of energy for decomposers, starting an imperative cycle in the supplement cycle. The benthic zone's wellbeing is significant for the general lake biological system, impacting water quality and giving environment to a different cluster of creatures.

Plants: The Oceanic Grounds-keepers:
Oceanic plants, going from lowered species like pondweeds to developing ones like cattails, assume a critical part in forming the lake environment. They act as oxygen

makers through photosynthesis, adding to the broke down oxygen content vital for fish and other oceanic life. Furthermore, plants settle the coastline, forestalling disintegration, and give living space and food to different creatures. The perplexing dance of green growth, phytoplankton, and bigger oceanic plants makes a lively submerged environment that impacts both the physical and organic parts of the lake.

Spineless creatures: The Microcosm of Variety:

The spineless creatures of a lake, including bugs, mollusks, and shellfish, structure a microcosm of variety inside the environment. These living beings frequently occupy the littoral zone, the region close to the coastline, where daylight enters and supports plant development. Spineless creatures assume vital parts in supplement cycling, going about as both decomposers and prey for bigger living beings. Mayflies, dragonflies, and water insects are only a couple of instances of the heap spineless creatures that add to the unpredictable food web of the lake.

Fish People group: Gatekeepers of the Amphibian Domain:

Fish, maybe the most apparent and financially huge occupants of lakes, structure complex networks represented by their natural jobs and connections. From ruthless species like pike and bass to planktivores like minnows, the variety of fish species adds to the steadiness and versatility of the environment. Fish feed on spineless creatures, control prey populaces, and, thusly, act as prey for flying predators, otters, and different carnivores. The outcome of fish populaces relies upon elements, for example, water temperature, broke up oxygen levels, and the accessibility of reasonable generating natural surroundings.

Avian Presence: Wings Over the Waters:

Birds, both transient and occupant, loan a dazzling presence to the lake environment. Waterfowl, like ducks and geese, track down asylum in the shallows and add to the dispersal of seeds. Swimming birds, similar to herons and egrets, chase after fish and spineless creatures in the shallows, while raptors fly above, prepared to plunge for a dinner. The lake's shores become fundamental settling destinations, and the occasional rhythms of avian relocation carry a powerful component to the biological system, featuring the interconnectedness of lakes and the more extensive scene.

Mammalian Inhabitants: Adjusting to the Water's Edge:

Warm blooded animals, adjusted to both amphibian and earthly life, cut their specialty along the water's edge. Beavers develop dams, changing the scene and making wetland territories that benefit various species. Otters, nimble swimmers, flourish with fish and spineless creatures, adding to the guideline of more modest sea-going populaces. Along the coastline, deer, raccoons, and different warm blooded creatures track down food and water, connecting the lake biological system to the encompassing earthly climate.

Microbial Players: Concealed Engineers of Equilibrium:

Microorganisms, frequently concealed however indispensable, are the engineers of supplement cycling and water cleaning inside the lake environment.

Microorganisms and different organisms separate natural matter, delivering supplements that fuel the development of plants and green growth. The microbial local area's structure and movement impact water quality, influencing the general soundness of the environment. Understanding the jobs of these minuscule creatures is fundamental for getting a handle on the multifaceted snare of life inside the lake.

Emanant Difficulties: Human Effect on Lake Biological systems:

As human exercises infringe upon normal scenes, lakes face a variety of difficulties that undermine their fragile environments. Contamination, environment obliteration, intrusive species, and environmental change are among the major problems influencing the wellbeing and equilibrium of lake biological systems. Supplement overflow from horticulture and metropolitan regions can prompt algal sprouts, upsetting the typical working of the lake. Obtrusive species, presented either purposefully or coincidentally, can outcompete local greenery, modifying the biological system's piece. Environmental change achieves shifts in temperature and precipitation designs, affecting the hydrology and generally speaking strength of lake biological systems.

Protection Endeavors: Safeguarding the Delicate Equilibrium:

Perceiving the significance of lake biological systems, preservation endeavors are in progress to protect their delicate equilibrium. Watershed the board, territory reclamation, and maintainable fishing rehearses intend to relieve human-actuated influences. Natural checking and research give experiences into the mind boggling associations inside lake biological systems, illuminating methodologies for preservation and economical asset the executives. Drawing in neighborhood networks in preservation drives encourages a feeling of stewardship, vital for the drawn out strength of lakes and their biological systems.

2.1 Description of the lake environment and its impact on the Common Loon

The lake climate, with its peaceful waters, beautiful scenes, and different biological systems, fills in as an enthralling setting for the existence of the normal nut case. This notable bird species, known for its eerie calls and exquisite developments on water, is unpredictably associated with the one of a kind elements of the lake. In this investigation, we dive into a point by point depiction of the lake climate, looking at its different parts and what they mean for the natural surroundings, conduct, and endurance of the normal nut case.

Actual Qualities of the Lake:

Lake Morphology:

The actual qualities of a lake essentially impact the existence of the normal nut case. Lakes come in different shapes and sizes, from little lakes settled in lush scenes to far reaching waterways outlined by rugged territory. Crackpots, with their inclination for bigger, more profound lakes, track down an ideal territory in these conditions. The morphology of the lake influences the dissemination of prey species, the accessibility of settling locales, and the general reasonableness of the natural surroundings for crackpot populaces.

Water Quality:

Water quality is a basic variable molding the lake climate. Crackpots, being piscivores, depend on the accessibility of clear, unpolluted waters to chase after fish. The clearness of the water impacts the bird's capacity to find prey, and the presence of contaminations can affect the soundness of the two crackpots and their oceanic prey. Supplement levels, broke down oxygen content, and the shortfall of pollutants add to the general prosperity of the lake environment, thusly influencing the normal nut case's scavenging achievement and conceptive achievement.

Biological Parts:

Amphibian Vegetation:

Amphibian vegetation, going from lowered plants to developing species, adds to the mind boggling embroidered artwork of the lake climate. These plants give essential natural surroundings to different oceanic organic entities, filling in as favorable places and haven for fish and spineless creatures. The presence of amphibian vegetation impacts the dispersion of prey accessible to crackpots and can affect the bird's capacity to participate in its trademark submerged quest for fish. Moreover, the vegetation assumes a part in molding the settling locales for nut cases, with rising plants frequently filling in as ideal areas for their ground homes.

Invertebrate Life:

The overflow and variety of invertebrate life in the lake are key to the normal crackpot's eating regimen, particularly during the rearing season. Bugs, scavangers, and different spineless creatures occupy the littoral zone, giving a promptly accessible food hotspot for crackpot chicks. The strength of the invertebrate populace is straightforwardly connected to the in general natural equilibrium of the lake, impacting the conceptive outcome of nut case matches and the endurance of their posterity.

Fish People group:

Fish are an essential part of the normal crackpot's eating regimen, and the sythesis of fish networks inside the lake is of fundamental significance. Lakes that help an assortment of fish animal types, including those liked by crackpots like roost and sunfish, offer an optimal rummaging climate. Changes in fish populaces, whether because of normal variances or human-actuated factors, can affect the searching progress of nut cases and their capacity to raise sound chicks.

Microbial Action:

Microorganisms assume a critical part in supplement cycling and water quality inside the lake. Microorganisms and different microorganisms separate natural matter, delivering supplements that help the development of green growth and other essential makers. The soundness of microbial networks impacts the supplement accessibility for amphibian plants and spineless creatures, by implication influencing the prey base for normal nut cases. Understanding the microbial elements inside the lake environment gives experiences into the more extensive biological cycles that shape the crackpot's living space.

Occasional Changes:

Occasional Fluctuation:

The lake climate goes through huge changes with the seasons, and these varieties significantly affect the normal nut case. Throughout the spring and mid year months, when lakes defrost and turn into a bustling place, nut cases participate in romance, settling, and raising their young. The overflow of prey, hotter water temperatures, and longer sunlight hours make ideal circumstances for nut case multiplication. Conversely, the fall and winter seasons bring difficulties, as lakes freeze in colder locales, restricting the accessibility of untamed water for searching. Understanding the occasional elements is urgent for fathoming the yearly life cycle and ways of behaving of the normal crackpot.

Movement Courses:

For specific crackpot populaces, movement is a critical part of their yearly cycle. Lakes serve as favorable places as well as visit focuses during relocation. Understanding the availability between various lakes along relocation courses is fundamental for protection endeavors, as interruptions to these territories can influence the general outcome of the nut case's yearly process. Protection drives that consider the whole transient pathway add to the safeguarding of the normal nut case's populaces.

Conduct Variations:

Settling Locales:

The lake climate shapes the settling conduct of normal nut cases. These birds fabricate ground homes, normally arranged on islands or segregated shores to limit earthbound predation gambles. The accessibility of appropriate settling locales impacts the reproducing outcome of nut cases, as aggravations or changes in the coastline can affect their capacity to effectively raise chicks. Protection endeavors frequently center around saving and keeping up with these basic settling natural surroundings.

Scrounging Systems:

Nut cases are all around adjusted to the lake climate, especially in their scrounging systems. Their smooth, smoothed out bodies and strong legs make them capable jumpers, empowering them to seek after fish submerged. The unmistakable, unpolluted waters of the lake are fundamental for their fruitful hunting tries. Concentrating on the scrounging ways of behaving of nut cases gives bits of knowledge into their dietary inclinations, the accessibility of prey, and the general soundness of the lake environment.

Human Effect:

Sporting Exercises:

Human exercises close by lakes can fundamentally influence the normal crackpot and its environment. Sporting exercises like sailing, fishing, and lakeside improvement can present aggravations that influence crackpot conduct. The presence of mechanized watercraft, specifically, may prompt home surrender or upset crackpot chicks, featuring the requirement for dependable sporting practices to limit human effect on these delicate birds.

Contamination and Living space Debasement:

The presentation of poisons, whether from rural overflow, modern release, or metropolitan turn of events, represents a serious danger to the lake climate and its occupants. Normal nut cases, being at the head of the sea-going pecking order, can collect pollutants in their bodies, prompting unfavorable wellbeing impacts. Living space corruption, including coastline adjustment and wetland obliteration, decreases the accessibility of appropriate settling locales and scrounging regions for crackpots.

Environmental Change Impacts:

Environmental change, with its related changes in temperature, precipitation examples, and ice cover, presents difficulties to the normal nut case and its lake territory. Changes in water temperature can impact fish populaces, influencing the crackpot's rummaging achievement.

Adjusted ice cover can influence the planning of rearing and relocation, disturbing the finely tuned yearly pattern of these birds. Understanding and alleviating the impacts of environmental change are critical for the drawn out protection of the normal crackpot and its lake climate.

Protection Endeavors:

Natural surroundings Security:

Preservation drives zeroed in on natural surroundings security are fundamental for shielding the lake climate and its occupants, including the normal nut case. Laying out and keeping up with safeguarded regions, for example, nature stores and untamed life asylums, guarantees that basic settling destinations, scavenging regions, and relocation visits stay undisturbed.

Natural Schooling:

Bringing issues to light about the significance of lakes and the normal crackpot inside neighborhood networks is a critical part of protection endeavors. Ecological schooling projects can assist with advancing dependable sporting practices, diminish contamination, and cultivate a feeling of stewardship for these fragile environments.

Examination and Checking:

Progressing exploration and observing projects are pivotal for figuring out the elements of the lake climate and the normal crackpot populaces. Long haul studies give important information on populace patterns, movement designs, and the effect of natural changes. This data shapes the establishment for proof based protection techniques.

2.2 Interconnectedness of the loon with other lake inhabitants

In the many-sided dance of the lake biological system, the normal nut case arises as a magnetic figure, complicatedly associated with a trap of associations with different occupants. This sea-going bird, with its frightful calls and effortless developments, assumes an imperative part in the interconnected embroidery of life around the lake. In this investigation, we disentangle the strings of the nut case's associations with different lake occupants, exhibiting the fragile equilibrium that supports this enthralling biological system.

Fish People group:

At the core of the crackpot's presence lies its relationship with fish networks abiding inside the lake. The crackpot is a piscivore, meaning it prevalently benefits from fish, especially species like roost, sunfish, and trout. The overflow and variety of fish straightforwardly influence the crackpot's scavenging achievement and, subsequently, its general wellbeing.

Thus, the nut case assumes a part in directing fish populaces by going after unambiguous species, adding to the environmental equilibrium inside the lake.

During the reproducing season, the nut case's reliance on fish turns out to be significantly more articulated as it looks for an ideal eating regimen to sustain its developing chicks. The accessibility of prey fish impacts the regenerative progress of crackpot matches, influencing the endurance and advancement of their posterity. The interconnectedness with fish networks features the fragile harmony among hunter and prey, profoundly shaping the way of behaving and methods for surviving of both the crackpot and the fish.

Invertebrate Life:

While fish structure a huge piece of the crackpot's eating regimen, spineless creatures likewise assume a urgent part in the bird's life cycle. During the reproducing season, particularly in the beginning phases when crackpot chicks are excessively little to devour fish, spineless creatures become a crucial food source. Bugs, scavangers, and other sea-going spineless creatures flourish in the littoral zones of lakes, where crackpots frequently scrounge.

The connection among nut cases and spineless creatures stretches out past simple food. The wellbeing and overflow of invertebrate life add to the general essentialness of the lake environment. Spineless creatures capability as fundamental connections in the established pecking order, interfacing essential makers to higher trophic levels. The crackpot, in its job as a buyer of spineless creatures, turns out to be important for this complex organization, supporting the interconnectedness of life inside the lake.

Oceanic Vegetation:

The presence of oceanic vegetation, going from lowered plants to emanant species, further develops the interconnected connections around the lake. These plants act as nurseries for fish, giving haven and favorable places to different species. Along these lines, the essentialness of fish populaces, a critical part of the nut case's eating regimen, is personally attached to the wellbeing of sea-going vegetation.

Also, the nut case's rearing propensities are complicatedly connected to the accessibility of appropriate settling locales given by new amphibian plants. Islands or disconnected shores decorated with developing vegetation become ideal areas for crackpot homes, offering assurance from earthbound hunters. The outcome of nut case proliferation is, consequently, interlaced with the overflow and variety of amphibian vegetation, stressing the sensitive equilibrium that describes the lake environment.

Flying predators and Hunters:

The normal nut case, in spite of its frightful calls and striking appearance, isn't absolved from the ruthless tensions of the lake climate. Flying predators, like birds and ospreys, share the skies over the lake with nut cases. These raptors might represent a danger to nut case chicks or even grown-up birds, making a perplexing powerful inside the avian local area.

The interconnectedness with flying predators stretches out past direct communications. The wealth of fish, a common asset, impacts the rummaging conduct of the two crackpots and raptors. Changes in fish populaces can, consequently, have flowing consequences for the whole avian local area, showing the extensive effect of interconnected connections in the lake environment.

On the other side, the normal nut case likewise assumes a part as a hunter. It rivals other waterfowl for assets and may try and participate in regional questions. Understanding the cooperations among crackpots and other bird species reveals insight into the complexities of avian connections inside the lake climate.

Mammalian Inhabitants:

Warm blooded creatures, both amphibian and earthbound, further add to the complicated embroidery of interconnected connections around the lake. Beavers, with their dam-building exercises, change the scene, making wetland natural surroundings that benefit different species. The changed climate, thusly, influences the scavenging conduct and settling selections of nut cases. Otters, lithe swimmers and fish trackers, share the oceanic space with crackpots and may impact fish populaces, by implication influencing the nut case's searching achievement.

Ashore, the presence of deer, raccoons, and different well evolved creatures impacts the coastline elements. These well evolved creatures might wander into the water's edge, possibly upsetting settling locales or influencing the accessibility of spineless creatures along the coastline. The collaborations among crackpots and earthbound warm blooded creatures feature the multifaceted connections that stretch out past the oceanic domain, stressing the interconnected idea of the lake biological system.

Microbial People group:

Microorganisms, frequently disregarded in the greatness of the lake climate, play a primary job in molding the interconnected connections inside the biological system. Microorganisms and different organisms take part in supplement cycling, separating natural matter and delivering fundamental supplements. The soundness of microbial networks impacts water quality, affecting the general prosperity of the lake and its occupants.

The normal nut case, as a top hunter, isn't excluded from the impacts of microbial exercises. The nature of water, represented by microbial cycles, impacts the accessibility of prey fish and spineless creatures. Understanding the microbial elements inside the lake biological system gives bits of knowledge into the more extensive environmental cycles that shape the living space of the normal nut case.

Human Effect:

The interconnected connections inside the lake climate face an imposing test - human effect. Human exercises, going from sporting pursuits to improvement and contamination, can disturb the fragile equilibrium of the environment, influencing the normal crackpot as well as all occupants of the lake.

Sporting sailing, for instance, presents aggravations that might disturb crackpot settling locales or cause pressure to birds during basic phases of their life cycle. Coastline improvement can modify territories, diminishing the accessibility of appropriate settling areas or scavenging regions. Contamination from horticultural overflow or modern release can taint the waters, influencing the wellbeing of fish populaces and, in this way, the nut case's eating routine.

Understanding the interconnectedness of the nut case with other lake occupants highlights the significance of capable human activities. Preservation endeavors that think about the more extensive environment, including fish, spineless creatures, plants, and other natural life, are fundamental for safeguarding the sensitive equilibrium that supports the normal nut case and its territory.

Preservation Suggestions:

Perceiving the complexities of interconnected connections inside the lake environment has significant ramifications for protection endeavors. Safeguarding the normal crackpot includes defending the actual bird as well as its reliant associations with different occupants of the lake.

Territory Protection: Protection drives should focus on the safeguarding of basic living spaces, including settling locales, rummaging regions, and movement visits. This includes safeguarding the nut case's prompt environmental factors as well as the more extensive lake climate, guaranteeing the accessibility of assets for all occupants.

Reasonable Asset The board: Feasible administration of fish populaces and other sea-going assets is pivotal for keeping up with the biological equilibrium. Practices, for example, mindful fishing and living space rebuilding add to the strength of the lake environment, helping both the normal crackpot and its kindred occupants.

Training and Effort: Ecological schooling assumes a critical part in cultivating mindfulness and comprehension of the interconnected connections inside the lake biological system. Connecting with neighborhood networks in preservation drives empowers mindful practices and advances a feeling of stewardship for these sensitive conditions.

Checking and Exploration: Continuous examination and observing projects give fundamental information to grasping the elements of the lake biological system. This data frames the reason for proof based protection methodologies, considering versatile administration to address arising difficulties and changes in the climate.

Alleviating Human Effect: Tending to the effect of human exercises on the lake biological system is central for the preservation of the normal crackpot. Guidelines and rules that advance capable drifting, limit coastline improvement, and lessen contamination add to the general prosperity of the lake and its occupants.

2.3 Poetic expressions of the symbiotic relationship between the loon and its habitat

In the captivating nexus of water and sky, a graceful expressive dance unfurls — a dance between the normal crackpot and its natural surroundings. This avian maestro, with its frightful calls and smooth developments, tracks down a musical reverberation inside the embroidery of lakes and peaceful waters. Artists, enthralled by this harmonious relationship, have woven sections that reverberation the expressive exchange between the crackpot and its amphibian sanctuary. This investigation submerges us in the idyllic articulations that enlighten the significant association shared by the nut case and its environment — a dance of reflections, an ensemble of sounds, and an everlasting verse scratched upon the watery stage.

Reflected Works:

As first light murmurs upon the lake, an orchestra of reflections is formed — a multifaceted poem that reflects the tastefulness of the normal crackpot. The tranquility of the water turns into a material whereupon the nut case paints its refrains, making a reflected poem in the early light. Each wave, a stroke of beautiful artfulness, as the nut case skims with a smoothness that rises above the limits among the real world and reflection.

The writer, a spectator of this reflected poem, considers the crackpot to be a wonderful draftsman, making stanzas with every development. The lake, in its responsive quietness, becomes both the crowd and the colleague — an immense mirror mirroring the crackpot's outline.

In this reflected poem, the writer examines the harmonious relationship, where the nut case turns into a residing section, and the lake, an immortal material catching the substance of its presence.

First light's Melodious Discourse:

With the coming of first light, the nut case participates in an expressive discourse with its environment. The air is injected with the frightful calls of the nut case, a melodic language that reverberates across the water. The lake, accordingly, turns into a thunderous chamber for this day break discourse — a melodious trade between the bird and its fluid environmental factors.

The writer, sensitive to the rhythm of the crackpot's calls, imagines a discussion between the avian artist and the responsive waves of the lake. Each call, a refrain that resounds through the morning air, makes an agreeable ensemble of sounds. The lake, in this expressive exchange, changes into a living composition, catching the melodic pith of the nut case's presence. The writer, an observer to this day break's expressive discourse, tracks down motivation in the cooperative trade between the crackpot and the full waters.

Nature's Haiku:

In the calm breaks of nature, a haiku unfurls — a brief articulation of the cooperative connection between the nut case and its territory. The crackpot, a singular figure on the lake, embodies the straightforwardness and class of a haiku. Its developments, similar to the painstakingly picked expressions of a haiku, convey a significant association with the quiet climate.

The writer considers this nature's haiku, where the nut case turns into the encapsulation of each painstakingly created syllable. The lake, with its intelligent surface and peaceful disposition, fills in as the material for this moderate work of art. In the quickness of a haiku, the writer catches the substance of the nut case's harmonious hit the dance floor with the lake — a dance that rises above the intricacies of language and resounds with the virtue of nature's stanza.

Dusk's Cinquain:

As dusk slides, a cinquain of shadows unfurls — a wonderful structure that reflects the transaction of light and murkiness. The crackpot, presently an outline against the diminishing sky, takes part in a cinquain of developments on the water's surface. The lake, accordingly, turns into a domain of shadows — a quiet accomplice in this sundown cinquain.

The artist, submerged in the blurring light, notices the crackpot's outline moving upon the intelligent material of the lake. Every development, a stanza in the cinquain, adds to the nuanced verse of sunset.

The lake, with its responsive waters, embraces the nut case as a loved colleague in the developing show of shadows. In the sundown's cinquain, the writer observes the consistent advantageous interaction between the nut case and its living space, where light and shadow participate in a graceful dance that rises above the limits of constantly.

Nighttime Melody:

Under the gleaming look of the moon, a nighttime melody unfurls — a melodious story that catches the crackpot's presence in the quietude of the evening. The frightful calls of the nut case reverberation across the still waters, making a melody that resounds through the twilight song. The lake, presently an intelligent stage for the nighttime number, turns into an idyllic shelter for the nut case's melodic articulations.

The writer, sensitive to the nighttime ensemble, imagines the nut case as a nighttime singer, singing sections that reverberation through the quiet evening. The lake, in its intelligent quiet, turns into an open crowd, enhancing the ethereal notes of the crackpot's song. In this nighttime song, the writer investigates the persevering through association between the crackpot and its living space, a relationship that twists underneath the divine gleam of the moon.

Reverberations of Isolation:

In snapshots of isolation, the writer considers the reverberations of the crackpot's presence — a discourse murmured across the boundlessness of the lake. The nut case, a lone writer in its oceanic safe-haven, travels through the reflected waters, leaving swells that reverberation the calm breaks of isolation. The lake, sweeping and peaceful, turns into a supply of reverberations — a demonstration of the cooperative relationship shared by the crackpot and the scrutinizing boundlessness of its territory.

The artist, submerged in these reverberations of isolation, perceives the significant association between the nut case and the quiet spread of the lake. Each wave, a murmured section, addresses the persevering through nature of the nut case's presence inside the hug of its watery home. In the reverberations of isolation, the writer finds an expressive story that unfurls in the calm minutes shared by the crackpot and the sweeping isolation of the lake.

Chapter 3

Seasons of the Loon

In the cadenced dance of nature, the normal crackpot arises as a charming hero, exploring the seasons with effortlessness and strength. Each period of the year delivers a particular tune in the existence of the nut case, from the lively tints of spring to the tranquil cover of winter. In this investigation, we set out on an excursion through the times of the nut case, unwinding the complexities of its ways of behaving, transformations, and difficulties as it explores the steadily changing embroidery of its natural surroundings.

Spring: The Enlivening Ensemble

As winter's frigid grasp surrenders its hold, the crackpot proclaims the appearance of spring with a frightful orchestra. Lakes defrost, and vast waters become the stage for the crackpot's romance customs. The male nut case, dazzling in its smooth reproducing plumage, participates in a movement of showcases — head shakes, warbling calls, and rich plunges. These exhibitions are graceful articulations as well as vital stages in the immortal dance of romance.

Settling locales become the crackpot's material in spring. Islands or segregated shores enhanced with rising vegetation are painstakingly picked for their detachment and security. The nut case, similar to a carefully prepared craftsman, creates its home, and soon the main eggs show up — a commitment of new life and coherence in the consistently spinning seasons.

The artist notices the nut case's springtime adventure — the enlivening of life reflected in the energetic plumage, the expressive romance calls, and the delicate expectation of fresh starts. Spring, for the crackpot, is a time of trust, a festival of life's recurrent resurgence.

Summer: Supporting New Life

With the glow of summer comes the bring forth of nut case chicks — a groundbreaking occasion that changes the quiet waters into a clamoring nursery. The nut case family, presently extended, sets out on an excursion of supporting and endurance. The chick's fleecy down fills in as a demonstration of the weakness of new life, yet under-neath this delicate outside lies the flexibility that describes the nut case's heredity.

The crackpot guardians, in a synchronized expressive dance, alternate defending the home and rummaging for food. The writer observes this parental organization — a two part harmony of commitment and obligation.

The lake, presently a venue for relational peculiarities, mirrors the shining solidarity of the crackpot family against the verdant setting of summer.

As the crackpot chicks develop, their wool feathers give method for sleeking plum-age, reflecting the progressive change of the lake climate. Summer turns into a section of development, investigation, and familial bonds — an expressive piece composed on the undulating surface of the lake.

Fall: The Fleeting Excellence

As summer's glow winds down, the nut case plans for the inescapable excursion toward the south. The lakes, once lively with the reverberations of nut case calls, presently witness a change in beat. The nut case's unpleasant cries, full with a dash of despairing, mark the takeoff from the mid year shelter.

The fall foliage fills in as an idyllic scenery to the crackpot's goodbye, making a scene of fleeting excellence. The artist catches the momentary minutes — the impression of pre-winter tints on the lake's surface, the outline of the crackpot against the evolving scene, and the mixed notes of its calls. Fall turns into a melancholic song, a preface to the nut case's relocation, and a sign of the transient idea of occasional changes.

Relocation: An Excursion Across Skylines

As fall develops, the nut case leaves on a transitory odyssey, exploring across immense distances to wintering grounds. The writer imagines the amazing excursion — the nut case's wings cutting through the fresh pre-winter air, its brings reverberating over lakes and waterways, and the aggregate soul of movement that ties crackpot populaces.

Movement is an orchestra of impulse and transformation, a beautiful articulation of endurance scratched into the crackpot's DNA. The artist examines the secrets of relocation — the route by divine prompts, the perseverance expected for long flights, and the aggregate heartbeat that guides crackpot networks across skylines. In the tremendous territory of relocation, the crackpot's occasional excursion turns into an adventure of versatility, solidarity, and the whole string of life.

Winter: Quietness on Frozen Waters

Winter covers the scene in peaceful quietness, and the nut case finds comfort in untamed water pockets in the midst of frigid fields. The lake, presently enhanced in a sparkling layer of snow, mirrors the serenity of winter. The nut case, having left its favorable places, looks for shelter in beach front waters or open lakes where the dance of ice fluid actually happens.

Winter is a time of thought for the crackpot — a relief from the requesting patterns of romance, nurturing, and relocation. The writer notices the nut case's colder time of year isolation — the quiet floats on bone chilling waters, the muffled calls that reverberate through frozen air, and the getting through soul that continues underneath the frigid facade.

In the quietude of winter, the nut case turns into a lone writer, forming sections on frozen waters. The lake, in its quieted rest, demonstrates the veracity of the crackpot's occasional transformation — the bird's flexibility, versatility, and the getting through association with its living space even notwithstanding winter's cruelest hug.

Interconnected Seasons: A Wonderful Continuum

The times of the crackpot structure a beautiful continuum — a story woven through the patterns of life, movement, and reflection. The artist examines this interconnected woven artwork — the development of new life in spring, the energetic shades of summer, the transient magnificence of fall, the transitory odyssey, and the quiet isolation of winter. Each season is a refrain, and the nut case's life, a melodious piece that reverberations through the evolving scenes.

The lake, as the quiet observer to these occasional changes, mirrors the significant association between the nut case and its environment. In the reflection of the water, the writer witnesses the immortal dance — a movement of variation, endurance, and the persevering through soul of the nut case. The lake, thus, turns into an idyllic material — a steadily changing background that highlights the magnificence and difficulties of each season.

3.1 Migration patterns and behavior of the Common Loon throughout the year

The normal crackpot, a great waterfowl animal varieties, sets out on a spectacular transient excursion that traverses immense distances and includes different living spaces. From its favorable places in the northern lakes to wintering areas in seaside waters, the nut case's movement is a mind boggling embroidery woven with organic rhythms, navigational ability, and natural versatility. In this broad investigation, we dive into the relocation examples and ways of behaving of the normal crackpot consistently, revealing the complexities of this astounding avian odyssey.

Occasional Elements:

The movement of the normal nut case is a unique cycle complicatedly attached to the evolving seasons. To comprehend the extensive extent of the nut case's transient examples, we will investigate its ways of behaving during each period of the year.

Spring Movement:

As winter surrenders its frigid grasp, the normal crackpot encounters the main stirrings of anxiety. Spring marks the beginning of the toward the north movement, flagging the re-visitation of favorable places settled in the northern lakes and freshwater bodies. This movement is set off by a blend of interior prompts, like hormonal changes, and outer variables like expanding day length.

In the beginning phases of spring relocation, the nut cases structure free rushes in their wintering regions, showing a helpful way of behaving that guides in exploring the sweeping distances they should cover. The artist imagines this aggregate exertion

— the crackpots coasting over vast waters, their calls reverberating as one as they start their excursion north.

Navigational impulses assume a significant part in the crackpot's movement. Research recommends that these birds are fit for using an assortment of direction prompts, including the World's attractive field and heavenly examples, to precisely explore. The writer mulls over the crackpot's divine route — their capacity to line up with the stars or utilize the World's attractive field as a compass, a heavenly dance that guides them towards their favorable places.

After arriving at their rearing destinations, frequently lakes encompassed by boreal woodlands, the nut cases participate in romance ceremonies and home structure exercises. The spring relocation, consequently, isn't simply an excursion yet an introduction to the many-sided patterns of reproducing and nurturing that characterize the crackpot's life.

Reproducing Season:

The landing in favorable places denotes the beginning of the crackpot's rearing season. The writer notices the crackpot matches participating in intricate romance shows, a movement of head-shaking, jumping, and warbling calls. These ways of behaving serve for the purpose of holding as well as a show of their reasonableness as mates.

The nut case's settling site is painstakingly picked for its disengagement and well-being, frequently on islands or separated shores embellished with emanant vegetation. The writer examines this choice interaction — a careful dance where the nut cases, as avian modelers, create homes that give a solid sanctuary to their posterity.

As the eggs are laid and the nut several alternates brooding them, the reproducing season turns into a time of given organization. The writer observes this familial expressive dance — the sharing of liabilities, the synchronized changes in home participation, and the expectation of new life. Reproducing season, entwined with the landing in favorable places, is a lovely recess in the crackpot's transitory excursion.

Summer Home:

Following fruitful settling, the nut case family stays in their late spring home, a peaceful lake encompassed by rich boreal scenes. The late spring months are portrayed by the supporting of crackpot chicks, the educating of fundamental basic instincts, and the continuous development of the youthful ones.

The writer catches the substance of summer home — the nut case family floating over the intelligent waters, the mournful calls of the chicks reverberating through the boreal backwoods, and the familial bonds reinforcing under the delicate daylight. The lake, in its mid year magnificence, turns into a beautiful background — a material painted with the shades of familial solidarity and the liveliness of life.

The nut case's way of behaving during this stage includes scavenging for food to support the developing chicks. Fish, especially little species like roost and sunfish, structure the essential eating routine. The writer notices the crackpot's fishing strategies — their capable jumps, submerged quest for prey, and the victorious reemerging with a catch. Summer home isn't just a time of supporting yet additionally a time of sharpening endurance senses.

Fall Relocation:

As summer advances to fall, the normal crackpot encounters one more call to relocation. The nut case's interior clock, receptive to unobtrusive changes in sunshine and ecological prompts, flags the looming takeoff from favorable places. The writer examines the despairing magnificence of fall movement — the nut case family saying goodbye to the recognizable lakes, the fresh harvest time air reverberating with the calls of leaving birds.

Fall movement, similar as its spring partner, includes really long travel. The nut cases leave on a toward the south excursion, exploring across lakes and streams in a journey for reasonable wintering grounds. The writer imagines this transient scene — the crackpots framing angular developments, the aggregate soul directing them through the evolving scenes.

As the crackpots venture toward the south, they might make stops on bigger lakes or waterfront waters. These interval destinations act as resting and rummaging regions, giving fundamental refueling to the requesting venture ahead. The artist observes these transient stops — the nut cases floating over the untamed waters, their calls reverberating with the changing shades of fall.

Winter Home:

The summit of fall relocation drives the normal nut case to its colder time of year home — a time of relative serenity contrasted with the unique periods of reproducing and movement. Beach front waters, bigger lakes, and marine conditions become the colder time of year asylum for crackpots looking for rest from the frosty northern winters.

The writer notices the crackpot's colder time of year home — a scene where the waterfront waves supplant the reflected quietness of northern lakes. The nut case, presently embellished in its non-rearing plumage, blends with other waterfowl species in these wintering regions. The colder time of year home is described by an emphasis on scrounging and endurance, as the nut cases adjust to an alternate arrangement of ecological difficulties.

Winter home isn't just a time of transformation yet in addition a chance for the nut cases to take part in friendly ways of behaving. The writer considers the colder time of year social occasions — the crackpots drifting in free runs, their brings making an ensemble over waterfront waters, and the aggregate versatility that characterizes their wintering networks.

Conduct Variations:

The normal nut case's movement isn't simply an actual excursion yet a progression of conduct variations that guarantee its endurance across different conditions. These transformations, sharpened over ages, exhibit the crackpot's wonderful capacity to explore, scrounge, and flourish despite evolving conditions.

Navigational Ability:

One of the most amazing parts of the nut case's movement is its navigational ability. The nut case depends on a blend of senses of direction and outside signals to navigate large number of miles with momentous accuracy.

Research recommends that the normal crackpot can see and use the World's attractive field for route. This inborn capacity permits them to keep an internal compass during both constantly, in any event, while flying over immense spans of vast water.

The writer wonders about the crackpot's divine route — a complex hit the dance floor with the stars and heavenly bodies. The nut case's capacity to utilize heavenly signs, for example, the place of the North Star, exhibits a profound association with the night sky, changing the transient excursion into a divine artful dance.

Scrounging Methodologies:

All through its transitory excursion, the nut case utilizes different scrounging methodologies adjusted to the attributes of its environmental elements. In the rearing season, the nut case's center movements to getting fish reasonable for supporting the developing chicks. The writer notices the nut case's fishing procedures — the subtle jumps, submerged quest for prey, and the quick reemerging with a catch.

In wintering regions, the nut case adjusts its searching propensities to marine conditions. Waterfront waters might offer an alternate cluster of prey, and the nut case changes its eating routine in like manner.

The writer mulls over the crackpot's colder time of year searching — the coordinated quest for fish underneath the sea's surface, a demonstration of their versatility in different environments.

Social Elements:

While nut cases are for the most part known for their lone nature, relocation and wintering periods achieve changes in their social elements. The artist observes the moving shared ways of behaving — the development of free runs during relocation, the colder time of year social affairs on waterfront waters, and the aggregate brings that resound over far reaching scenes.

These social cooperations fill different needs, including security, correspondence, and the trading of data about searching open doors. The writer mulls over the nut case's collective presence — a fragile harmony among isolation and friendliness that improves their possibilities of endurance in various periods of movement.

Difficulties and Dangers:

The transient excursion of the normal nut case is loaded with difficulties, both regular and anthropogenic. Understanding these difficulties is urgent for preservation endeavors pointed toward saving the respectability of the nut case's relocation and guaranteeing the maintainability of its populaces.

Normal Difficulties:

The crackpot faces normal difficulties all through its transient process. Storms, unfriendly weather patterns, and predation are innate dangers that can influence the progress of movement. The writer examines the nut case's versatility — the capacity to weather conditions storms, explore through violent skies, and endure despite normal difficulties.

Moreover, the accessibility of reasonable visit destinations during relocation is critical. Changes in land use, natural surroundings corruption, or aggravations here can disturb the nut case's capacity to rest and refuel during long excursions. The writer ponders the sensitive harmony between the normal moves and the nut case's capacity to adjust — a demonstration of the many-sided dance among bird and climate.

Anthropogenic Dangers:

Human exercises present huge dangers to the normal nut case's transitory excursion. The adjustment of reproducing environments, contamination of lakes and waterfront waters, and impacts with electrical cables or designs are among the anthropogenic difficulties looked by crackpot populaces.

The artist examines the effect of human exercises — the infringement on reproducing destinations, the contamination that corrupts the nature of lakes, and the crashes that upset the transient flight. Preservation endeavors become vital in alleviating these dangers, guaranteeing that the crackpot's transient courses stay undisturbed and its environments stay flawless.

Protection Endeavors:

Protecting the transient examples and ways of behaving of the normal crackpot requires coordinated preservation endeavors. The artist considers the significance of protecting the environments, limiting anthropogenic effects, and encouraging a comprehension of the crackpot's natural importance.

Territory Protection:

Safeguarding the rearing, settling, and wintering environments of the normal crackpot is key to its preservation. Preservation associations and policymakers assume a pivotal part in laying out and upholding guidelines that safeguard the uprightness of these environments. The writer mulls over the meaning of undisturbed favorable places, flawless lakeshores, and secure wintering regions — a wonderful vision of environments safeguarded for the crackpot's transitory excursion.

Local area Commitment:

Drawing in neighborhood networks in preservation drives is a fundamental part of protecting the normal nut case. The writer imagines an amicable conjunction among networks and crackpot territories — a common obligation regarding the protection of lakes, adherence to mindful drifting practices, and a pledge to diminishing contamination. Through people group mindfulness and inclusion, the artist sees the potential for maintainable practices that benefit the two people and crackpots.

Observing and Exploration:

Progressing exploration and checking programs give fundamental information to figuring out the elements of the crackpot's movement. The artist thinks about the meaning of logical undertakings that disclose the secrets of heavenly route, disentangle the complexities of scrounging ways of behaving, and evaluate the effect of ecological changes on nut case populaces. Research frames the reason for proof based protection techniques, taking into account versatile administration to address arising difficulties.

Relieving Human Effect:

Tending to the effect of human exercises on the nut case's transient process is fundamental for its protection. Guidelines and rules that advance dependable sailing, limit coastline improvement, and decrease contamination add to the general prosperity of the crackpot and its natural surroundings. The writer considers the fragile harmony between human exercises and biological protection — a dance where capable practices become the movement for a feasible future.

3.2 Poetic exploration of the loon's experiences during different seasons

In the regular cadence of the seasons, the normal nut case arises as a lovely hero, exploring the moving scenes and adjusting to the nuanced embroidery of evolving climates. Each season lays out a one of a kind picture of the nut case's encounters, from the dynamic quality of spring's romance ceremonies to the tranquil isolation of winter's rest. In this graceful investigation, we dig into the spirit of the crackpot, mulling over its excursion through the expressive focal point of the evolving seasons.

Spring: An Expressive dance of Romance

In the enlivening hug of spring, the crackpot arises as a ballet artist on the reflected phase of northern lakes. The writer imagines this scene — a rich male enhanced in reproducing plumage, participating in a movement of romance. Head shakes, warbling calls, and synchronized plunges become sections in the nut case's springtime ensemble.

The lake, actually defrosting from winter's frosty sleep, turns into a graceful material where the crackpot records its yearning. The writer notices the nut case's romance customs — a dance that reflects the thriving existence of the time. The female nut case, a quiet dream, answers the melodious advances, and together they make a two part harmony reverberating across the water's surface.

The romance isn't simple science; it is a graceful story of association, want, and the commitment of new life. The writer considers the nut case's springtime expressive dance — an amicable suggestion that proclaims the appearance of warmth and the repeating mood of life.

Summer: Supporting Tunes

As spring rises above into the lively embroidery of summer, the nut case finds its safe house on disconnected lakes embraced by boreal backwoods. The writer imagines the crackpot family — a peaceful scene where guardians guide wool chicks through the undulating waters. The calls of the nut case, tormenting and melodic, become the soundtrack of summer's peacefulness.

The lake, presently an intelligent surface reflecting the verdant scenes, turns into the stage for the crackpot's sustaining tunes. The artist notices the nut case family floating through the water, their synchronized developments repeating the familial bonds produced in the cauldron of summer.

Summer is a poem written in the gleaming shades of lake reflections, a demonstration of the crackpot's obligation to the congruity of life. The writer ponders the crackpot's mid year home — a safe-haven where the air is interspersed with calls, and the fluid sections of the lake support the nut case family in a wonderful hug.

Fall: A Melancholic Takeoff

In the progress from summer's glow to fall's fresh hug, the crackpot encounters a clashing excursion. The writer ponders the crackpot family saying goodbye to the natural lakeshores, the despairing calls reverberating in the harvest time air. Fall turns into an impactful song of flight.

As the nut cases structure angular arrangements in the sweeping sky, the writer imagines the aggregate soul of movement — the instinctual pull toward far off waters. The lake, presently embellished in the transient magnificence of fall foliage, turns into a quiet observer to the nut case's goodbye — a melodious takeoff from the familial summer residence.

The writer catches the quintessence of fall relocation — a transitory scene painted in the shades of evolving scenes. The nut case's process turns into a powerful moral story, a movement that repeats the general subject of goodbyes and the certainty of progress.

Winter: Isolation on Frozen Waters

As fall surrenders its hold to winter's hug, the crackpot looks for shelter in seaside waters and open lakes. The writer imagines the crackpot, presently embellished in non-rearing plumage, exploring through frigid spreads. Winter turns into a time of isolation and consideration.

The lake, frozen and quieted, mirrors the quietude of winter. The nut case, in its colder time of year home, turns into a singular writer coasting over frozen waters. The writer considers the crackpot's colder time of year isolation — a time of rest, reflection, and perseverance despite winter's chill.

Winter is a work of distinct magnificence — the crackpot's presence an outline against the snow-hung scene, the muffled calls resounding through still air. The artist sees the crackpot's flexibility, adjusting to the requests of winter while keeping up with the persevering through association with its sea-going domain.

Repeating Reflections: An Idyllic Continuum

In the repeating dance of the seasons, the crackpot's encounters unfurl as refrains in an everlasting sonnet — a story that rises above individual minutes and meshes into the texture of nature's ceaseless mood. The writer considers this recurrent reflection — the crackpot's process through spring's romance, summer's supporting hug, fall's melancholic takeoff, and winter's scrutinizing isolation.

The lake, ever-receptive to the crackpot's presence, mirrors the changing states of mind of the seasons. In spring, it reflects the enthusiasm of romance; in summer, it supports the crackpot family in its fluid stanzas; in fall, it catches the momentary magnificence of takeoff; and in winter, it turns into a quiet material for the nut case's colder time of year isolation.

The writer sees the interconnectedness of these encounters — an idyllic continuum where each season is a verse, and the crackpot's life, an expressive structure that resounds through the moving scenes. In mulling over this recurrent reflection, the writer tracks down motivation in the persevering through dance between the crackpot and living space — a dance rises above time and repeats the everlasting rhythm of nature.

The Writer's Appearance:

As the writer considers the crackpot's encounters through various seasons, they become a mirror mirroring the immortal subjects of life, change, and interconnectedness. The crackpot, with its balletic romance, supporting tunes, melancholic takeoff, and scrutinizing isolation, turns into a dream for stanzas that rise above the limits of the avian world.

The lake, in its intelligent quietness, turns into the wonderful material where the crackpot's encounters are painted with the brushstrokes of evolving seasons. The writer mulls over the lake's job — a quiet comrade, a responsive accomplice, and an immortal observer to the nut case's excursion through the idyllic embroidery of nature.

In the impression of the crackpot's encounters, the writer finds the magnificence of avian life as well as the significant verse that rises up out of the cozy association among bird and environment. The crackpot's excursion through the seasons turns into an illustration for the human experience — a sign of the repeating idea of presence, the certainty of progress, and the persevering through soul that endures even despite changes.

As the writer's appearance converges with the expressive story of the crackpot, they track down comfort in the immortal dance — a dance that rises above the vaporous limits of seasons and makes an amicable orchestra where the nut case's encounters become sections carved into the aggregate memory of the normal world.

3.3 Reflections on how poets use the changing seasons as metaphors in loon-themed poetry

In the sensitive dance among nature and verse, the normal nut case arises as an enrapturing muse, rousing writers to wind around stanzas that resound with the evolving seasons. The crackpot, with its unpleasant calls, effortless developments, and occasional relocations, turns into an idyllic vessel through which the subtleties of the regular world are investigated. In this broad investigation, we dig into the intelligent imaginativeness of artists who tackle the allegorical force of changing seasons in their nut case themed verse, uncovering the advantageous interaction between avian excellence and the timeless rhythm of nature.

Spring: Illustration for Recharging and Romance

In the domain of crackpot themed verse, spring fills in as a figurative harbinger of recharging and romance. As the ice withdraws from northern lakes, writers imagine the crackpot's return as an expressive resurgence — a resurrection of life reflected in the sparkling waters. The writer mulls over the crackpot's romance ceremonies, seeing them as stanzas recorded on the pages of an occasional work.

The crackpot's frightful calls become illustrations for the enlivening earth, reverberating through the timberlands and across the waters like a beautiful ensemble. In this season, the lake turns into a figurative stage — a theater where the nut case participates in an expressive dance of romance. The artist considers this allegorical dance — the waves on the lake's surface, the transaction of daylight and shadow, and the nut case's outline carved against the material of spring.

As the crackpot matches participate in a dance of romance, writers attract equals to the lively tints of sprouting vegetation. The lake's shores become figurative nurseries, enhanced with emanant vegetation that reflects the nut case's settling locales. The writer ponders the nut case's decision of separated areas — a similitude for the hallowed spaces where life is sustained and progression is commended.

Spring, in crackpot themed verse, turns into an illustration for the everlasting pattern of life — a season where the nut case's romance isn't just an organic basic however a representative articulation of nature's enduring restoration. The writer, through sections that resound with the rhythms of spring, catches the embodiment of the nut case's allegorical hit the dance floor with the evolving season.

Summer: Illustration for Supporting and Congruity

As spring changes into the glow of summer, nut case themed verse digs into the figurative lavishness of this season — a period of supporting and concordance. The writer imagines the nut case family coasting over serene waters, every development a figurative stroke on the material of the lake.

Summer turns into a similitude for familial bonds — a season where the crackpot guardians, as graceful overseers, guide their wool chicks through the undulating reflections. The writer ponders the crackpot's mid year home as a figurative safe house — an asylum where the air is loaded up with the unpleasant songs of calls, and the lake's surface turns into a figurative support.

The lake, in the mid year representation, changes into a fluid work — an encapsulation of peacefulness and familial solidarity. The nut case's fishing trips become representations for the difficulties of life as a parent, the dexterity of plunges a figurative dance of endurance. The artist ponders the nut case's scrounging techniques — the submerged quest for prey, the victorious reemerging, and the exchange of information to the future.

Summer, in crackpot themed verse, turns into a similitude for the sensitive harmony between the nut case and its environment. The lake's intelligent surface turns into a figurative mirror — a demonstration of the familial bonds and the amicable concurrence among bird and climate. The writer, through refrains that reverberation with the quietness of summer, catches the allegorical pith of the crackpot's sustaining tunes.

Fall: Analogy for Progress and Flight

As the glow of summer respects the fresh hug of fall, nut case themed verse embraces the figurative subtleties of change and flight. The writer imagines the nut case family saying goodbye to the natural lakeshores — a takeoff that turns into a similitude for the certainty of progress.

Fall, in nut case themed verse, fills in as a similitude for the transient excellence of life. The changing foliage turns into a figurative scenery — a material painted with the short lived tones of flight. The writer considers the nut case's transitory excursion as a figurative journey — an odyssey through evolving scenes, full with the widespread topic of changes.

The angular arrangements of nut cases in the pre-winter sky become similitudes for aggregate soul and shared fates. The writer imagines the nut case's takeoff — a melancholic song reverberating through the fall air, a figurative goodbye to the familial summer home. The lake, presently enhanced in the powerful magnificence of fall, turns into a figurative observer to the crackpot's transitory odyssey — a quiet comrade to the changing parts of avian life.

Fall, in crackpot themed verse, turns into an illustration for the repeating idea of presence — a season where takeoff isn't an end yet a preface to the following part. The writer, through stanzas that reverberate with the despairing excellence of fall, catches the allegorical quintessence of the nut case's transient process and the all inclusive subject of advances.

Winter: Analogy for Isolation and Examination

In the tranquil quiet of winter, crackpot themed verse considers the figurative isolation and examination of the nut case. The writer imagines the nut case coasting over frozen waters — a lone writer exploring the cold scope. Winter turns into a similitude for rest — a season where the crackpot withdraws into scrutinizing isolation.

The frozen lake, in the figurative winter scene, turns into an intelligent mirror — a material for the crackpot's calm examination. The writer mulls over the crackpot's colder time of year home as a figurative shelter — a safe-haven where the calls are quieted, and the nut case turns into a lone artist forming refrains on frozen waters.

Winter, in nut case themed verse, turns into an illustration for strength — a season where the crackpot perseveres through the chill and adjusts to the requests of a frozen territory. The writer considers the crackpot's colder time of year quietness — a figurative recess in the avian story, a break from the requesting patterns of romance, nurturing, and movement.

The nut case, presently embellished in non-rearing plumage, turns into a similitude for contemplation and perseverance. The writer notices the nut case's colder time of year isolation — a figurative float on freezing waters, a quiet float on the material of the lake. Winter turns into a work of obvious excellence — a figurative reflection on the persevering through soul that continues underneath the frigid facade.

Recurrent Reflections: A Graceful Continuum

In the rich embroidery of nut case themed verse, the changing seasons act as similitudes that string through the avian story, making a beautiful continuum. Each season turns into a figurative verse, and the nut case's encounters, an expressive structure that reverberates through the moving scenes. The artist, through figurative reflections on the evolving seasons, ponders the interconnectedness among bird and territory.

The lake, as the quiet observer to the nut case's allegorical excursion, mirrors the significant association between the avian drifter and its current circumstance. The writer mulls over the allegorical embodiment of this association — the lake's responsiveness to the crackpot's presence, the figurative reflections that reflect the changing mind-sets of the seasons, and the getting through dance among bird and territory.

In the allegorical embroidery of crackpot themed verse, the artist finds the excellence of avian life as well as the significant figurative verse that rises out of the personal association among bird and territory. The crackpot's figurative excursion through the seasons turns into a similitude for the human experience — a sign of the repeating idea of presence, the certainty of progress, and the persevering through figurative soul that endures even despite figurative changes.

The Writer's Appearance:

As the writer ponders how writers utilize the changing seasons as illustrations in crackpot themed verse, they wind up drenched in a figurative ensemble — an investigation of avian magnificence and the everlasting rhythm of nature. The nut case, with its unpleasant calls, balletic romance, familial songs, transient flights, and pensive isolation, turns into a figurative dream for stanzas that rise above the limits of the avian world.

The artist examines the allegorical wealth of each season — the resurrection of spring, the sustaining amicability of summer, the despairing excellence of fall, and the thoughtful isolation of winter. Through allegorical reflections on the evolving seasons, the writer finds the figurative subtleties of avian life as well as the allegorical strings that mesh the nut case's encounters into the more extensive story of nature's figurative continuum.

In the figurative dance between the nut case and the evolving seasons, the writer tracks down motivation — a dream that reverberates with the figurative rhythms of life, change, and interconnectedness. Through figurative verse, the crackpot's figurative excursion turns into an immortal allegorical song — a getting through orchestra that reverberations through the allegorical passageways of the regular world.

Chapter 4

The Language of the Loon

In the immense breadth of lakes and streams, the normal nut case arises as a vocal virtuoso, its unpleasant calls reverberating across the intelligent surfaces of northern waters. The language of the nut case, a melodic and complicated correspondence framework, fills in as a window into the avian world's secrets. In this broad investigation, we dig into the subtleties of the language of the nut case, translating the significance behind its calls, warbles, and tremolos. Through a vivid excursion into the avian vocabulary, we look to disentangle the complexities of how nut cases convey, explore, and express the substance of their reality.

Vocal Collection: The Crackpot's Phonetic Ensemble

The crackpot's vocal collection is an orchestra of sounds, each call and warble conveying explicit implications and filling particular informative needs. To comprehend the language of the crackpot is to set out on a sonic excursion, where the avian notes resound with the rhythms of the normal world.

Tremolo: The Articulate Vibration

The tremolo, a quick and shuddering call, is a primary component of the crackpot's language. This vocalization is frequently compared to chuckling, yet its motivation stretches out past simple articulation of delight. The writer ponders the tremolo — a sonic sign that reverberations across the lake's surface, flagging regional limits and declaring the crackpot's presence in its oceanic domain.

The language of the nut case, as communicated through the tremolo, turns into a figurative statement of proprietorship — a declaration of the lake's fluid field as the crackpot's expressive space. The writer considers the tremolo's nuanced rhythm — a phonetic vibration that resounds through the nut case's watery realm.

Cry: The Deep Discourse

The howl, an eerie and melancholic call, is a strong component of the nut case's vocal collection. The writer examines the cry — a heartfelt monologue that resonates through the boreal timberlands, making a hear-able embroidery woven with reverberations of isolation and longing.

The cry turns into a representation for the crackpot's existential articulation — a lovely talk that exemplifies the embodiment of avian isolation. The writer investigates the howl's reverberation — a reminiscent etymological gadget that rises above the limits of the avian world and imparts the nut case's close to home scene to mindful audience members.

Warble: The Romance Structure

The warble, a progression of rising and dropping notes, is a romance call that assumes an essential part in the language of the crackpot. The writer imagines the warble — a romance sythesis that unfurls like a heartfelt piece across the intelligent waters of the lake.

The warble turns into an illustration for avian romance — a melodious articulation that reverberations through the boreal scenes, flagging the nut case's longing for friendship. The writer considers the warble's complex tune — a semantic dance that entwines with the nut case's balletic romance ceremonies, making an orchestra of adoration on the northern lakeshores.

Hoots and Groans: The Nighttime Murmurs

Hoots and groans, low-recurrence vocalizations, act as the nut case's nighttime murmurs — a language that unfurls under the front of obscurity. The writer considers these quieted expressions — a secretive etymological collection that adds profundity to the crackpot's informative ensemble.

The language of hoots and groans turns into a figurative exchange between nut cases — a murmured discussion that explores the domains of haziness and reverberations through the quiet evening. The writer investigates the nighttime subtleties of nut case correspondence — a phonetic embroidery woven with stifled takes note of, a demonstration of the crackpot's flexibility to various open settings.

Logical Correspondence: Translating the Language of Cooperation

Past the singular vocalizations, the language of the nut case reaches out into a perplexing snare of relevant correspondence. From regional questions to familial securities, nut cases utilize a different scope of informative ways of behaving to explore their social and natural scenes.

Regional Questions: The Sonic War zones

Regional questions among crackpots frequently manifest as vocal fights — an ensemble of tremolos and moans that resonate across the lake. The writer ponders these sonic conflicts — a figurative war zone where regional limits are drawn and protected through the expressiveness of crackpot language.

The language of regional debates turns into a representation for avian discretion — a discussion helped out through the unpredictable rhythm of calls. The writer considers the sonic limits scratched into the lake's surface — a regional guide depicted by the expressiveness of nut case vocalizations.

Family Correspondence: The Melodic Bond

Inside the nut case nuclear family, correspondence takes on a nuanced and melodic structure. The calls and warbles become a method for building up familial bonds, planning exercises, and guaranteeing the security of chicks. The writer imagines the family correspondence — a melodic bond that rises above the outer layer of the lake and resounds through the boreal scenes.

The language of familial correspondence turns into a similitude for solidarity — an amicable orchestra where each note addresses a familial association. The writer ponders the crackpot guardians' organized endeavors — a wonderful dance that unfurls on the water's surface and guarantees the prosperity of the nut case descendants.

Mate Acknowledgment: The Murmured Assertions

Crackpot mates perceive each other through the inconspicuous subtleties of their calls — a murmured certification that rises above the boundlessness of the lake. The writer ponders this mate acknowledgment — a phonetic code that fills in as an illustration for avian constancy and the getting through connections between crackpot matches.

The language of mate acknowledgment turns into a figurative statement of responsibility — a murmured insistence that reverberations through the boreal woods. The writer investigates the unpretentious varieties in mate acknowledgment calls — a lovely exchange that reaffirms the crackpot matches' association in the midst of the extensive oceanic scene.

Navigational Correspondence: The Sonic Compass

During movement or route across far reaching waters, nut cases use their language as a navigational device. The writer imagines this navigational correspondence — a sonic compass that guides nut cases through the divine embroidery of the night sky and the immeasurability of untamed water.

The language of navigational correspondence turns into an illustration for heavenly dance — a movement where the nut case lines up with the stars and the World's attractive field. The writer ponders the nut case's divine route — a lovely excursion directed by the expressiveness of calls and the intrinsic comprehension of the avian dictionary.

Ecological Versatility: The Language of Endurance

The language of the nut case isn't just a method for correspondence yet additionally an instrument for natural versatility. Because of evolving conditions, crackpots utilize various vocalizations and open techniques to explore their environmental elements.

Hunter Evasion: The Quiet Signals

When confronted with possible hunters, nut cases show a way of behaving known as "penguin pose" — a quiet sign of weakness that conveys a condition of readiness. The writer ponders this quiet correspondence — a representation for the versatile methodologies utilized by crackpots to explore the difficulties of predation.

The language of hunter evasion turns into a representation for endurance — a murmured signal that rises above the perceptible domain and imparts through the nut case's stance. The writer considers the quiet signals scratched into the nut case's way of behaving — a figurative dance that guarantees the avian virtuoso's wellbeing even with possible dangers.

Natural Changes: The Versatile Rhythm

In light of natural changes, for example, moving toward tempests or aggravations, crackpots adjust their vocalizations and conduct. The writer imagines this versatile rhythm — a representation for the crackpot's responsiveness to the moving temperaments of the normal world.

The language of versatile rhythm turns into a figurative indicator — an avian orchestra that repeats the changing environmental circumstances. The writer considers the crackpot's capacity to peruse the natural signals — a wonderful dance that guarantees the avian virtuoso's strength even with dynamic scenes.

Social Importance: The Language of Human Translation

The language of the crackpot reaches out past the avian domain, charming human minds and moving translations in different social settings. From native fables to present day writing, the nut case's calls have turned into a dream for artists, narrators, and specialists the same.

Native Old stories: The Reverberations of Folklore

In native societies, the nut case holds a huge spot in folklore and old stories. The writer considers the reverberations of native folklore — a social reverberation where the language of the crackpot becomes interlaced with the stories of creation, change, and the interconnectedness of every single residing being.

The language of native legends turns into an illustration for social legacy — a wonderful continuum where the nut case's calls are avian articulations as well as representative reverberations of genealogical insight.

The writer considers the crackpot's job in native narrating — a figurative extension that interfaces the avian world with the rich embroidery of human social creative mind.

Artistic Motivation: The Writer's Dream

In writing and verse, the crackpot's language fills in as a dream for expressive and reminiscent sections. The writer imagines the crackpot as a wonderful dream — a wellspring of motivation that rises above the limits of the avian world and tracks down reverberation in the persuasiveness of human language.

The language of scholarly motivation turns into a representation for the harmonious connection among writers and the regular world — a dance where the nut case's calls are converted into sections that reverberation the excellence, secret, and despairing of presence. The writer considers the crackpot's job in molding scholarly scenes — a figurative presence that improves the human story with avian persuasiveness.

Imaginative Portrayal: The Visual Poetics

Visual specialists frequently draw motivation from the language of the crackpot, making canvases, figures, and different works of art that catch the embodiment of avian correspondence. The writer mulls over the visual poetics — a representation for the crackpot's extraordinary ability to rise above hear-able domains and become a visual orchestra.

The language of imaginative portrayal turns into a representation for the transaction between avian magnificence and human innovativeness — a dance where the crackpot's calls are converted into strokes, tones, and structures that resound with the tasteful sensibilities of human onlookers. The writer considers the nut case's visual poetics — a figurative material where the avian virtuoso turns into a dream for visual articulations of the normal world.

Preservation Suggestions: Deciphering the Language for Security

The language of the crackpot conveys social and tasteful importance as well as functional ramifications for protection endeavors. Understanding and deciphering the subtleties of crackpot correspondence can add to the conservation of their natural surroundings and the prosperity of nut case populaces.

Human Unsettling influence: Deciphering Pressure Signs

Human exercises, like sailing and coastline advancement, can upset crackpot living spaces. The writer considers the translation of stress signals — a representation for grasping the language of the nut case because of anthropogenic unsettling influences.

The language of stress signals turns into a representation for preservation mindfulness — a wonderful exchange that urges people to decipher the unobtrusive prompts of nut case correspondence and change their ways of behaving to limit unsettling influences. The artist ponders the nut case's capacity to impart pressure — an avian account that addresses the fragile harmony between human exercises and the conservation of crackpot natural surroundings.

Environment Quality: Interpreting Vocal Wellbeing

The vocal soundness of crackpots can act as a mark of living space quality. Changes in vocalizations might flag ecological stressors, contamination, or modifications in the amphibian biological system. The writer mulls over the disentangling of vocal wellbeing — an illustration for understanding the language of the nut case as an impression of the prosperity of its natural surroundings.

The language of vocal wellbeing turns into an illustration for natural stewardship — an idyllic discourse that underlines the interconnectedness between the nut case's calls and the biological uprightness of its sea-going domain. The writer considers the nut case's vocal articulations as ecological gauges — a poem that highlights the significance of saving perfect natural surroundings for the avian virtuoso.

Environmental Change: Adjusting to Modified Soundscapes

Environmental change can adjust the soundscapes of nut case natural surroundings, influencing the spread and gathering of their vocalizations. The writer imagines the variation to modified soundscapes — a similitude for the language of the crackpot developing because of changing natural circumstances.

The language of transformation turns into a similitude for flexibility — a wonderful discourse that investigates the crackpot's capacity to explore through changed hear-able scenes. The writer considers the nut case's versatile reactions to environmental change — a piece that highlights the significance of protection techniques that address the more extensive natural difficulties looked by crackpot populaces.

4.1 Study of the loon's distinctive calls and communication methods

In the serene lakes and streams of northern locales, the eerie calls of the normal crackpot resound through the tranquility, making a melodic ensemble that repeats the avian virtuoso's presence. The investigation of the crackpot's unmistakable calls and specialized strategies reveals a rich embroidery of avian language, a nuanced dictionary that fills in for of route, social cooperation, and ecological variation. In this investigation, we dig into the complexities of the crackpot's vocalizations, translating the implications behind its tremolos, howls, warbles, and other unmistakable calls. The review reveals insight into the open ability of the nut case, uncovering how these calls act as a passage to grasping the avian world's secrets.

Tremolo: The Articulate Mark of the Nut case

One of the most particular calls of the nut case is the tremolo, a fast and trembling vocalization frequently compared to chuckling. The investigation of the tremolo uncovers its multi-layered job in crackpot correspondence. Scientists have seen that the tremolo fills in as a self-assured statement of regional limits. At the point when two crackpots experience each other in shared waters, the tremolo turns into a sonic limit marker, flagging each bird's case over a particular district.

The concentrate further demonstrates that the tremolo isn't restricted to regional debates; it likewise works as an overall articulation of the nut case's presence. During serene minutes on the lake, the nut case might produce tremolos as an approach to confirming its regional possession and conveying its presence to different crackpots nearby.

Besides, the tremolo's recurrence and force can shift, giving scientists extra experiences. The review has shown that nut cases will generally utilize more lively tremolos when confronted with expected dangers or aggravations, demonstrating the versatility of this particular call to various informative settings.

Moan: The Melancholic Song of Isolation

The moan is one more famous vocalization of the crackpot, a frightful and melancholic call that reverberations across the boreal scenes. The investigation of the howl dives into its open importance, uncovering a call that reaches out past regional declarations and fills in as an impactful articulation of the crackpot's personal state.

Specialists have seen that the howl is frequently utilized by crackpots during snapshots of isolation or partition from their mate or posterity. It turns into a profound monologue that resounds through the quietness of the lake, conveying a feeling of longing and close to home profundity. The cry, as the review recommends, isn't only a hear-able articulation however a piercing impression of the crackpot's existential experience.

Moreover, the howl has been seen during seasons of aggravation or seen dangers. In such cases, the crackpot might radiate a progression of howls, flagging an elevated condition of watchfulness or misery. The investigation of the howl as a reaction to ecological boosts reveals insight into the crackpot's capacity to convey its personal and situational mindfulness through this particular call.

Warble: The Romance Organization

The warble is a romance call novel to the male nut case, and its review uncovers a captivating part of crackpot correspondence related with the rearing season. The warble is described by a progression of climbing and slipping notes, making a resonant piece that fills in as a romance presentation to draw in expected mates.

Specialists have broadly concentrated on the warble with regards to crackpot romance customs. The review demonstrates that the warble is certainly not a lone execution yet rather a piece of an arranged romance dance. The male crackpot takes part in a progression of showcases, including head shakes, neck stretches, and plunges, with the warble filling in as the hear-able highlight of this romance ensemble.

The warble isn't just a method for drawing in a mate yet additionally a type of mate acknowledgment. The review proposes that crackpot matches may involve varieties in their warbles to distinguish and reaffirm their bond with one another. The warble, in this specific situation, turns into an unmistakable component of avian romance language, a pleasant articulation of adoration and association.

Hoots and Groans: The Nighttime Murmurs

Hoots and groans are low-recurrence vocalizations produced by nut cases, and their review reveals a feature of crackpot correspondence that reaches out into the domain of the nighttime. While the hoots and groans may not be pretty much as prominent as the daytime calls, they assume a huge part in the crackpot's open collection during evening hours.

The investigation of hoots and groans recommends that these nighttime murmurs fill different needs, including correspondence between nut case matches and relatives. Dissimilar to the more prominent calls like the tremolo or howl, hoots and groans are frequently unpretentious and low-pitched, permitting nut cases to keep in touch with one another without making potential hunters aware of their presence.

Scientists have noticed that hoots and groans become more articulated during specific exercises, like taking care of or when nut cases are in nearness. The investigation of these nighttime vocalizations reveals insight into the versatility of crackpot correspondence to various ecological circumstances and the significance of keeping up with social bonds during evening exercises.

Relevant Correspondence: Figuring out the Subtleties

The investigation of the nut case's particular calls goes past individual vocalizations, enveloping a more extensive comprehension of relevant correspondence. Crackpots use their brings in unambiguous circumstances, adjusting their vocalizations to pass various messages accordingly on to differing conditions.

Regional Debates: Sonic Limits

The investigation of crackpot correspondence with regards to regional debates uncovers a refined arrangement of sonic limits. At the point when two crackpots experience each other in shared waters, they take part in a vocal fight, frequently highlighting the tremolo as the essential weapon.

The review shows that the power and span of the tremolo trades are straightforwardly connected to the degree of animosity and the assurance of every crackpot to state its regional case.

The concentrate further features the job of different calls, like the moan, in regional debates. The moan, with its melancholic tones, may act as a supplemental articulation of strength or as a sign of the crackpot's close to home state during these showdowns.

Family Correspondence: Melodic Bond

In the nuclear family, the investigation of crackpot correspondence discloses a melodic bond communicated through facilitated calls and vocalizations. Crackpot guardians and chicks participate in a complicated transaction of calls that supports familial bonds, coordinate exercises, and guarantee the security of the posterity.

The review shows that particular calls, like delicate hoots or groans, might be utilized by nut case guardians to speak with their chicks without drawing in unnecessary consideration. These unobtrusive calls make a melodic security that rises above the outer layer of the lake and reverberates through the boreal scenes, guaranteeing powerful correspondence inside the nuclear family.

Mate Acknowledgment: Murmurs of Loyalty

The investigation of crackpot correspondence with regards to mate acknowledgment uncovers a nuanced arrangement of murmured certifications. Crackpot mates perceive each other through unpretentious varieties in their calls, making a sonic mark that builds up their bond.

Scientists have seen that nut case matches may take part in two part harmonies, planning their calls to make an agreeable orchestra. The review recommends that mate acknowledgment calls assume a significant part in reaffirming the devotion between nut case matches, permitting them to explore the far reaching waters while keeping in touch and association.

Navigational Correspondence: Sonic Compass

During movement or route across immense water bodies, the investigation of nut case correspondence reveals a sonic compass that directs these avian drifters. The calls utilized during movement are particular from those utilized in different settings, showing a specific open procedure.

Scientists have noticed that nut cases might utilize explicit calls to keep in touch with one another during relocation, making a sonic compass that aids route. The review proposes that this navigational correspondence depends on the crackpot's capacity to decipher and answer the changing hear-able signals of the vast water and the heavenly woven artwork above.

Natural Flexibility: Calls as Versatile Reactions

The investigation of the nut case's particular calls underlines the versatility of these vocalizations to different natural circumstances and difficulties. From hunter evasion to answering changes in the soundscape, crackpots exhibit a noteworthy capacity to adjust their specialized strategies to guarantee endurance.

Hunter Aversion: Quiet Signals

The review uncovers that nut cases utilize explicit ways of behaving and calls as quiet signals when confronted with possible hunters. The "penguin act," a quiet sign of weakness, is a non-vocal specialized strategy that the crackpot uses to convey an elevated condition of sharpness without making hunters aware of its presence.

The review proposes that these quiet signals are a critical part of the nut case's hunter evasion methodology, permitting the bird to explore through possibly risky circumstances without drawing in pointless consideration. This versatile reaction features the significance of non-vocal specialized strategies in the avian collection.

Natural Changes: Versatile Rhythm

Crackpots exhibit a versatile rhythm in light of changes in their current circumstance. The review demonstrates that ecological shifts, like moving toward tempests or aggravations, evoke explicit changes in crackpot vocalizations and conduct.

The review proposes that nut cases might modify the recurrence or force of their brings because of natural changes, making a versatile rhythm that imparts their consciousness of moving circumstances. This versatile correspondence procedure permits nut cases to explore through powerful scenes and answer successfully to the difficulties presented by an evolving climate.

Preservation Suggestions: Deciphering Calls for Assurance

Understanding the subtleties of the crackpot's unmistakable calls has huge ramifications for protection endeavors. The investigation of nut case correspondence gives important experiences into the soundness of their environments, the effect of human exercises, and the general prosperity of crackpot populaces.

Human Aggravation: Deciphering Pressure Signs

The review recommends that nut cases emanate explicit calls as pressure signals because of human aggravations. Sailing, coastline improvement, and other anthropogenic exercises can upset crackpot natural surroundings, and specialists have noticed changes in nut case vocalizations as marks of pressure.

Deciphering these pressure signals becomes pivotal for protection endeavors, permitting specialists and traditionalists to distinguish regions where human exercises might be adversely influencing crackpot populaces.

The review underlines the significance of limiting aggravations to guarantee the prosperity of nut cases in their regular living spaces.

Natural surroundings Quality: Vocal Wellbeing as a Marker

The investigation of nut case vocalizations gives an original way to deal with evaluating natural surroundings quality. Changes in the recurrence, force, or construction of crackpot calls might act as signs of ecological stressors, contamination, or modifications in the sea-going environment.

Moderates can utilize the review's discoveries to decipher the vocal wellbeing of crackpots and recognize expected dangers to their environments. By checking changes in vocalizations, specialists gain a harmless device for evaluating the general soundness of nut case populaces and the environments they occupy.

Environmental Change: Versatile Reactions to Modified Soundscapes

Environmental change presents difficulties to the acoustic scenes of crackpot territories, and the review proposes that nut cases show versatile reactions to adjusted soundscapes. Changes in vocalizations might mirror the crackpot's capacity to explore through developing ecological circumstances.

Protection procedures that consider the versatile reactions of crackpots to environmental change can add to the drawn out conservation of these avian populaces. The review highlights the significance of considering the powerful idea of the acoustic conditions in protection arranging and the executives.

4.2 Poetic interpretations of the loon's vocalizations

In the ethereal dusk of northern lakes, the frightful calls of the normal crackpot weave a wonderful ensemble, rising above the limits of avian language to turn into a melodious embroidery of nature's emotive composition. Writers, dazzled by the perplexing tunes of the crackpot, track down motivation in the unmistakable vocalizations that reverberation through the boreal scenes.

Tremolo: A Shuddering Suggestion

The tremolo, that fast and trembling call frequently compared to giggling, turns into a shuddering suggestion in the writer's stanzas. The writer imagines the tremolo as a statement scratched onto the outer layer of the lake — a decree of the crackpot's fluid sway. In lovely language, the tremolo changes into a dance of waves, each quiver resounding with the beat of the nut case's pulse. It is a statement of presence, a smooth wave that crosses the lake and waits in the aggregate memory of the writer's stanzas.

Howl: A Deep Talk

The howl, with its melancholic tone, changes into a deep talk in the writer's thoughts. The writer imagines the howl as an existential articulation — a piercing talk that reverberations across the water's surface. In the howl, the nut case turns into a solitary singer, entertaining the twilight night with a song that catches the quintessence of isolation. The writer, receptive to the cry's sad notes, makes an interpretation of the avian speech into refrains that investigate the profundities of longing and the despairing magnificence of the crackpot's presence.

Warble: A Romance Piece

The warble, a romance call embellished with climbing and dropping notes, transformations into a romance piece in the writer's creative mind. The writer imagines the warble as a balletic structure — an ensemble of affection reverberating across the water's breadth. With each note, the crackpot turns into a lovely maestro, arranging a dance of romance that unfurls on the intelligent phase of the lake. The warble turns into an illustration for avian sentiment, and the writer makes an interpretation of this romance work into stanzas that praise the immortal dance of affection.

Hoots and Groans: Nighttime Murmurs

Hoots and groans, the low-recurrence murmurs of the crackpot, change into nighttime murmurs in the writer's nocturne. The writer imagines the hoots and groans as a murmured discussion between crackpots, unfurling underneath the twilight overhang. In these nighttime murmurs, the crackpot turns into a ghostly writer, forming sections that reverberate through the quiet evening. The writer catches the nuance of these avian mumbles, meshing them into a graceful story that rises above the diurnal limits.

Interchange of Calls: Avian Piece

The exchange of calls, the sonic discourse of crackpots on shared waters, advances into an avian work in the artist's refrains. The writer imagines the crackpots as co-writers of a piece, each call a verse in the melodious structure of the lake. The tremolo, cry, warble, hoots, and groans become wonderful similitudes — an aggregate articulation of the nut case's excursion through the seasons and the subtleties of its avian presence.

In the lovely understandings of the crackpot's vocalizations, the writer turns into an interpreter of nature's songs. Each call, a stanza in the avian epic, reverberates with the writer's spirit, moving refrains that reverberation the excellence, secret, and despairing of the nut case's presence. The crackpot's vocalizations, in the possession of a writer, become more than sounds — they become a persevering through ensemble, an immortal work, and an expressive dance that catches the substance of the avian virtuoso.

4.3 Exploring the idea of language and communication in nature poetry

In the immense span of nature, where each stir of leaves, each twitter of a bird, and each wave on a lake communicates in its very own language, writers have tracked down an unending wellspring of motivation. Nature verse, as a sort, dives into the perplexing embroidery of the normal world, trying to unwind the subtleties of language and correspondence that exist past the human domain. This investigation stretches out past simple perception, welcoming artists to become interpreters of the basic discoursed that unfurl in the wild. In this exhaustive investigation, we dive into the possibility of language and correspondence in nature verse, disentangling the advantageous connection among writers and the smooth articulations of the regular world.

1. **The Quiet Language of Scene**
    The Scene as Beautiful Letters in order

    Nature, in its quiet greatness, turns into a graceful letters in order — a vocabulary composed across mountains, waterways, and glades. The writer examines the language of the scene, where each component, from the transcending tops to the wandering streams, imparts a story that rises above human words. Mountains might remain as quiet sentinels, their tough shapes a work of versatility. Streams might mumble stanzas of never-ending movement, an unending beautiful current that carves stories into the world's material. The writer turns into an etymological map maker, planning the forms of the land with sections that reverberation the quiet language of the scene.

The Murmuring Breeze as Stanza

The breeze, an enduring writer, turns into a vehicle for the murmurs of nature. Through the stirring of leaves and the delicate stroke of a breeze, the breeze verbalizes stanzas that cross the open spaces. The writer pays attention to the breeze's murmured poems, making an interpretation of the unobtrusive rhythm into lines that hit the dance floor with the transient magnificence of air moving. The language of the breeze turns into a similitude for the transient idea of presence — a murmuring update that nothing in nature is static, and each second is a verse in the continuous sonnet of life.

The Sun and Moon: Heavenly Verse

The sun and moon, heavenly illuminating presences, participate in a grandiose discussion that unfurls across the sky. The sun, with its brilliant sections, writes light upon the earth, while the moon, with its silver murmurs, winds around nighttime works in the embroidery of the evening.

The artist thinks about the divine discourse, interpreting the language of constantly into refrains that catch the everlasting dance of light and shadow. Through this inestimable verse, the normal world turns into a heavenly composition, and the writer turns into a translator of the sun and moon's glowing language.

2. **The Greenery: An Avian and Botanic Dictionary**

The Ensemble of Birds: Avian Canticles

Birds, the avian virtuosos, add to nature's ensemble with their sweet calls and complex chorales. Every species flaunts an unmistakable vocalization, a one of a kind note in the avian canticle. The writer turns into an ornithological lyricist, investigating the subtleties of each bird's language — from the songbird's sweet melody to the crow's cawing rhythm. In these avian sections, the writer uncovers the tales of romance, an area, and movement, changing the language of birds into a melodious vocabulary that adds profundity to the regular story.

Flower Murmurs: Botanic Ditties

The language of blossoms, communicated through varieties, fragrances, and structures, turns into a botanic song that writers disentangle. Every petal and leaf is a stanza in the botanical ensemble, a nuanced articulation of the plant's presence. The artist thinks about the murmurs of blooms, deciphering the energetic tints and aromas into stanzas that summon the vaporous magnificence of the herbal world. Through this investigation, the writer turns into a green artist, disentangling the plant melodies that beauty glades, backwoods, and nurseries.

The Dance of Bugs: Microcosmic Minuets

Bugs, with their unpredictable developments and humming discoursed, add to the microcosmic minuets of nature's dance. The shuddering wings of butterflies, the productive murmur of honey bees, and the vaporous effortlessness of dragonflies become articulations of the insectile language. The writer drenches themselves in the entomological works, catching the nuanced movement of bugs through stanzas that commend the microcosmic minuets of the regular world.

3. **Human instinct Discourse: Wonderful Convergences**
Biological Exchanges: Human and Nature as Conversational Accomplices
Nature verse frequently fills in as a vehicle for an exchange among people and the climate. The writer turns into a middle person in the environmental discussion, investigating the sensitive exchange among humankind and the normal world. Ecological difficulties, protection endeavors, and the effect of human exercises become sections in this continuous exchange.

Through nature verse, the writer considers the outcomes of human activities on the scene, making an interpretation of the ecological story into refrains that call for stewardship and amicability.

The Seasons: Nature's Yearly Epic
The evolving seasons, a common legendary in nature's story, become a wonderful investigation of recurrent changes. Each season, from the blooming of spring to the quieted tranquility of winter, contributes refrains to the yearly epic. The writer turns into an occasional recorder, winding around refrains that catch the states of mind, tones, and feelings of every worldly part. Through this investigation, nature and mankind take part in an exchange where the seasons become shared representations, reverberating with the human experience.

The Brilliant and the Stylish: Nature's Personal Range
Nature, in its magnificent greatness, summons a scope of feelings that writers convert into sections. The immensity of mountains, the serenity of lakes, and the magnificence of woodlands become a profound range, each scene painting a material of feelings. The writer turns into a close to home interpreter, catching the amazement, miracle, and worship enlivened essentially's heavenly magnificence. Through these stanzas, the writer participates in an exchange with the brilliant, articulating the unutterable through the language of feelings.

4. **Nature Verse as Ecocritical Talk**
Interconnectedness and Ecocentrism: A Lovely Declaration
Nature verse frequently fills in as a vehicle for ecocritical talk — an intelligent investigation of humankind's interconnectedness with the regular world. The artist considers the biological ramifications of human activities, making an interpretation of natural worries into sections that supporter for ecocentrism. Through this graceful declaration, nature turns into a hero, and the writer turns into a backer for the characteristic worth of the climate. The language of nature verse develops into a call for biological care, underlining the interconnectedness of every living being.

Natural Activism: Refrains as Promotion
Nature verse, in its investigation of language and correspondence, changes into an amazing asset for ecological activism. The writer turns into a supporter, using sections to bring issues to light about natural issues, preservation endeavors,

and the critical requirement for economical practices. Through this promotion, nature verse turns into an energizing cry, rousing perusers to draw in with the normal world and partake in the aggregate work to safeguard the climate.

5. **Idyllic Customs: An Embroidery of Styles and Structures**

Haiku and Moderation: Catching Nature's Embodiment

Haiku, a customary Japanese idyllic structure, embodies the craft of catching nature's pith in a moderate design. In only a couple of lines, haiku writers distil the excellence of scenes, the fleeting idea of seasons, and the effortlessness of normal peculiarities. The writer turns into an expert of moderation, utilizing succinct stanzas to inspire significant associations with the normal world.

Sentimentalism: Nature as Wonderful Dream

The Heartfelt custom, with its accentuation on the brilliant and the close to home reaction to nature, impacts numerous nature artists. Writers inside the Heartfelt practice celebrate nature as a grand dream, winding around stanzas that investigate the close to home profundity and profound reverberation tracked down in regular scenes. The writer turns into a heartfelt visionary, deciphering the magnificence of nature through sections that resound with the emotive force of the eminent.

Ecopoetry: Voices for the Climate

Ecopoetry arises as an unmistakable class inside the more extensive domain of nature verse, zeroing in expressly on biological topics and ecological cognizance. Ecopoets draw in with the language of nature to address contemporary environmental difficulties, offering stanzas that act as both creative articulations and suggestions to take action. The writer turns into an ecopoet, exploring the convergences of language, nature, and activism to add to a developing scholarly development that supporters for the climate.

Chapter 5

Human Interaction and Conservation

Preservation isn't only a question of safeguarding scenes and saving natural life; it is profoundly interlaced with human connection. The fragile harmony between human exercises and the common habitat has significant ramifications for the soundness of environments, biodiversity, and the general prosperity of our planet. This thorough investigation digs into the diverse connection between human collaboration and protection, inspecting the difficulties, amazing open doors, and developing ideal models that shape our way to deal with defending the World's environmental trustworthiness.

1. **Authentic Viewpoints on Human Association and Preservation**
   Native Insight and Conventional Natural Information
   By and large, native networks play had a significant impact in protection through their profound comprehension of the regular world and supportable asset the board rehearses. Customary Environmental Information (TEK) has been gone down through ages, offering important experiences into agreeable conjunction with nature. The investigation of native preservation rehearses gives an establishment to contemporary protection endeavors, underscoring the significance of regarding and consolidating nearby information in biodiversity security procedures.
   Early Preservation Developments and the Introduction of Natural Morals
   The nineteenth and mid twentieth hundreds of years saw the rise of preservation developments, prodded by worries about the exhaustion of regular assets and the effects of industrialization. Figures like John Muir and Theodore Roosevelt supported for the safeguarding of flawless scenes, prompting the foundation of public parks and the introduction of the natural preservation ethic. This period laid the preparation for a more extensive comprehension of humankind's liability towards nature, making way for the improvement of ecological morals and a more all encompassing way to deal with protection.

2. **Current Difficulties: Anthropogenic Tensions on Environments**
   Urbanization and Territory Discontinuity
   Fast urbanization represents a huge test to protection endeavors, prompting territory discontinuity and misfortune. As human populaces grow, regular scenes are changed into metropolitan regions, upsetting biological systems and secluding untamed life populaces. Understanding the elements of urbanization and carrying out systems to relieve its effect on biodiversity are fundamental parts of contemporary preservation.

   Environmental Change and Worldwide Effect
   Human-actuated environmental change has arisen as one of the most squeezing difficulties to preservation. Climbing temperatures, outrageous climate occasions, and moving climatic examples undermine biological systems around the world. Preservation endeavors should adjust to address the effects of environmental change, requiring techniques for both relief and variation. Reasonable practices, environmentally friendly power sources, and worldwide collaboration are vital to relieving the worldwide effect of environmental change on biodiversity.

   Overexploitation and Unreasonable Asset Use
   The tenacious interest for normal assets, driven by populace development and impractical utilization designs, adds to overexploitation and consumption of biodiversity. Overfishing, deforestation, and poaching are among the dangers energized by extreme asset use. Protection requires tending to the underlying drivers of overexploitation, advancing maintainable practices, and cultivating a capable demeanor towards asset utilization.

   Contamination and Natural Debasement
   Human exercises, especially modern cycles and the utilization of poisons, add to natural debasement. Contamination of air, water, and soil adversely influences environments and stances dangers to natural life and human wellbeing. Protection endeavors should incorporate measures to lessen contamination, execute cleaner advancements, and backer for arrangements that focus on natural wellbeing.

3. **Protection Practically speaking: Techniques and Ideal models**
   Safeguarded Regions and Biodiversity Areas of interest
   Laying out safeguarded regions stays a basic procedure for preservation. Public parks, natural life stores, and marine safe-havens assume a significant part in protecting biodiversity and giving territories to jeopardized species. Recognizing and saving biodiversity areas of interest — regions with especially elevated degrees of species wealth and endemism — offers a designated way to deal with protection arranging.

   Local area Based Preservation
   Perceiving the essential job of neighborhood networks in protection, local area based approaches have acquired conspicuousness. Drawing in nearby occupants

in preservation drives cultivates a feeling of stewardship and guarantees that protection rehearses line up with local area needs. Effective models incorporate local area oversaw saves and cooperative tasks that offset preservation objectives with financial contemplations.

Supportable Turn of events and Protection

Coordinating preservation with feasible improvement is a change in outlook that looks to accommodate natural security with human prosperity. Manageable advancement objectives focus on friendly, monetary, and ecological variables, recognizing the interconnectedness of these angles. Protection rehearses that advance supportable asset use, ecotourism, and local area strengthening add to an all encompassing and impartial way to deal with ecological stewardship.

Corporate Protection Drives

Progressively, partnerships are perceiving their job in ecological protection and executing manageability drives. Corporate preservation includes taking on harmless to the ecosystem works on, supporting protection projects, and adding to biodiversity insurance. The coordinated effort among organizations and protection associations can drive positive change, showing the way that financial turn of events and preservation can exist together.

4. **Preservation Morals and Instruction: Molding Attitudes for Maintainability**

Natural Instruction and Mindfulness

Building a maintainable future requires ingraining natural mindfulness and morals since the beginning. Ecological training programs assume a vital part in encouraging a feeling of obligation towards nature, sustaining educated and reliable residents who effectively add to protection endeavors. Incorporating ecological training into school educational programs and advancing public mindfulness crusades are fundamental parts of shaping earth cognizant social orders.

Protection Morals and Values

Moral contemplations are basic to preservation navigation. Preservation morals go past reasonable systems to envelop the qualities that guide our communications with the regular world. Ideas like natural worth, biocentrism, and profound environment impact moral structures for protection, accentuating the inborn worth of every living being and biological systems. A moral way to deal with preservation guarantees that human connections focus on the prosperity of the climate and its occupants.

5. **Mechanical Developments in Protection**

Remote Detecting and GIS Advances

Headways in remote detecting and Geographic Data Framework (GIS) advancements have changed preservation observing and arranging. Satellite symbolism, robots, and GIS planning empower specialists to survey changes in land cover, screen natural life populaces, and distinguish basic preservation regions. These mechanical instruments upgrade the accuracy and adequacy of preservation procedures.

Hereditary Innovations for Species Protection

Hereditary innovations, like DNA examination and conceptive advances, assume a crucial part in animal types preservation. Protection geneticists utilize these instruments to survey hereditary variety, distinguish people for reproducing projects, and battle issues like inbreeding. Even with environment misfortune and environmental change, hereditary advancements add to the safeguarding of imperiled species and the rebuilding of undermined populaces.

Resident Science and Publicly supporting

Resident science drives influence the force of public cooperation to gather information and add to preservation research. Drawing in residents in checking untamed life, recording biodiversity perceptions, and taking part in natural undertakings upgrades the extension and size of protection endeavors. Publicly supporting stages empower cooperative information assortment, transforming ordinary people into important supporters of logical exploration.

6. **Difficulties and Contentions in Human-Driven Protection**

Human-Untamed life Struggle

The concurrence of people and untamed life frequently prompts clashes, especially in regions where human exercises infringe upon normal natural surroundings. Human-natural life struggle presents difficulties to both preservation and local area prosperity. Methodologies for alleviating clashes incorporate the advancement of viable natural life the executives plans, local area commitment, and the execution of innovations like impediments and fencing.

Eco-The travel industry and Its Effects

While eco-the travel industry can add to preservation by giving monetary motivating forces to safeguarding normal regions, it likewise raises worries about its possible adverse consequences. Expanded human presence in biologically delicate regions can prompt natural surroundings aggravation, untamed life stress, and adjusted environments. Adjusting the advantages of eco-the travel industry with the requirement for severe protection measures requires cautious preparation and the executives.

Preservation Imperialism and Native Privileges

The burden of protection strategies disregarding the privileges and viewpoints of native networks raises moral worries. Protection imperialism, described by hierarchical methodologies that ignore neighborhood information and independence, can prompt social deletion and foul play. Recognizing the freedoms of native people groups and coordinating their points of view into protection systems is critical for moral and compelling preservation.

7. **Future Possibilities and Worldwide Participation**

Worldwide Joint effort for Worldwide Protection

Protection challenges reach out past public lines, requiring worldwide participation. Worldwide preservation drives, like the Show on Organic Variety (CBD) and peaceful accords, highlight the significance of cooperative endeavors to resolve issues like biodiversity misfortune and environmental change. Shared liability and information trade structure the establishment for powerful worldwide preservation systems.

Imaginative Financing Models for Preservation

Getting monetary assets is difficult for preservation endeavors. Imaginative subsidizing models, including public-private organizations, influence money management, and preservation finance components, are arising as elective methodologies. Utilizing different money sources guarantees the maintainability of preservation drives and encourages a monetary biological system that upholds ecological stewardship.

Innovation and Information Driven Protection Arranging

The coordination of state of the art advances and information driven approaches will keep on molding the fate of protection arranging. Man-made consciousness, AI, and large information examination empower more exact demonstrating, checking, and dynamic in preservation. The combination of mechanical developments with customary natural information improves the flexibility and adequacy of preservation procedures.

5.1 Impact of human activities on the Common Loon population

The unpleasant calls of the Normal Nut case reverberation across northern lakes, making a hear-able embroidered artwork that meshes into the texture of the wild. In any case, this famous bird, with its unmistakable high contrast plumage and suggestive cries, faces a horde of difficulties because of human exercises. As human impact reaches out into distant environments, the fragile equilibrium that supports the Normal Nut case populace is progressively unwinding. This investigation dives into the diverse effect of human exercises on Normal Crackpots, looking at the ramifications for their reproducing environments, searching grounds, and by and large prosperity.

1. **Living space Misfortune and Discontinuity**
   Coastline Improvement: A Hazardous Interruption
   One of the essential dangers to Normal Crackpots is the infringement of human advancement along coastlines. As waterfront properties thrive with cabins, resorts, and never-ending suburbia, the nut cases find their normal territories contracting. The aggravation brought about by development, the adjustment of the coastline, and the expansion in human presence upset the quiet settling locales that the nut cases rely upon for reproducing.

   The deficiency of perfect settling regions not just straightforwardly influences the quantity of accessible settling destinations yet additionally lifts the gamble of human-crackpot clashes. Nut cases, delicate to unsettling influence during the settling season, may forsake their homes if more than once upset by human exercises, prompting diminished conceptive achievement and a decrease in the general populace.

Territory Discontinuity: Disconnection Means something bad

The fracture of living spaces represents an extra danger to Normal Nut case populaces. As lakeshores become specked with structures, the once interconnected water bodies that gave broad searching and settling reason for nut cases become divided. This separation can restrict the birds' capacity to track down reasonable rearing destinations, access food assets, and explore across their regular reach.

Nut cases, known for their constancy to explicit rearing domains, face difficulties when these regions are undermined by natural surroundings fracture. The confined development brought about by divided territories can prompt expanded rivalry for restricted assets, a decrease in hereditary variety, and a general decrease in the flexibility of Normal Nut case populaces.

2. **Water Quality and Contamination**

   Oceanic Contamination: A Quiet Danger Beneath the Surface

   The strength of the sea-going environments in which Normal Crackpots dwell is complicatedly connected to their prosperity. Sadly, human exercises frequently bring contaminations into these conditions, representing a quiet danger to crackpot populaces.

   Substance toxins from modern releases, horticultural spillover, and neighborhoods can pollute the lakes and waterways where Normal Crackpots feed. These contaminations, going from weighty metals to pesticides, amass in the oceanic pecking order, eventually influencing the crackpots at the highest point of this chain.

   Tainted water bodies can prompt the bioaccumulation of poisons in fish, an essential food hotspot for nut cases. As the nut cases consume these sullied fish, they incidentally ingest hurtful substances, prompting a peculiarity known as biomagnification.

   The effect on the Normal Crackpot populace can appear in conceptive disappointments, debilitated resistant frameworks, and, in outrageous cases, mortality.

3. **Sporting Unsettling influences and Human-Crackpot Clashes**

   Drifting and Watercraft: An Approaching Danger

   The ubiquity of sporting drifting and water-based exercises adds one more layer of intricacy to the difficulties looked by Normal Nut cases. Nut cases are exceptionally delicate to unsettling influences during their settling and reproducing seasons, and the presence of mechanized watercraft represents a huge danger.

   Boat wakes can flood nut case homes arranged near coastlines, prompting home surrender and the deficiency of eggs or chicks. Also, rehashed aggravations by boats can cause pressure, redirect the consideration of grown-up nut cases from basic nurturing obligations, and disturb the delicate equilibrium of their regenerative endeavors.

   Human-Nut case clashes emerge when boaters accidentally approach settling locales or neglect with comply to rules for capable drifting around crackpot environments. Public mindfulness crusades and the foundation of defensive guidelines are fundamental to moderate these struggles and encourage an agreeable concurrence between sporting exercises and crackpot preservation.

4. **Environmental Change and Its Flowing Impacts**
Increasing Temperatures and Natural surroundings Movements
The ghost of environmental change creates a long shaded area over Normal Crackpot populaces. Climbing temperatures, adjusted precipitation examples, and changes in ice cover significantly influence the amphibian biological systems that crackpots call home. These environment prompted movements can prompt the change of conventional reproducing and scavenging living spaces, making an outpouring of difficulties for the nut cases.

The planning of ice dissolve and the accessibility of vast water are basic elements for Normal Crackpots during their reproducing season. Changes in ice cover can upset laid out designs, influencing the planning of crackpot appearance and settling. The bungle between the planning of bring forth and the pinnacle accessibility of food assets can endanger the endurance of nut case chicks, prompting decreased conceptive achievement.

5. **Preservation Endeavors and Moderation Systems**
Environment Insurance and Rebuilding
Endeavors to shield Normal Crackpot populaces depend on territory assurance and rebuilding drives. Safeguarding lacking coastlines, keeping up with normal settling locales, and laying out safeguarded regions are essential parts of territory preservation. Cooperative endeavors including preservation associations, government organizations, and nearby networks can add to the formation of powerful protection measures.

Rebuilding projects that emphasis on moderating territory fracture and improving network between water bodies can assume a crucial part in supporting Normal Nut case populaces. These ventures might include the evacuation of hindrances, the formation of untamed life halls, and the execution of scene arranging that thinks about the natural requirements of the nut cases.

Public Mindfulness and Capable Amusement
Public mindfulness crusades are fundamental instruments for alleviating the effect of sporting aggravations on Normal Nut case populaces. Instructing boaters, fishers, and lakeside land owners about the environmental responsiveness of crackpot territories and the significance of capable entertainment can cultivate a culture of protection.

Laying out and upholding guidelines that depict proper good ways from settling destinations, speed limits for watercraft, and occasional limitations during basic times of nut case reproducing can assist with limiting human unsettling influences. Associations between protection associations, government organizations, and sporting networks can improve the viability of such drives.

Water Quality Observing and Contamination Control

To address the dangers presented by water contamination, powerful water quality observing projects are fundamental. Ordinary appraisals of foreign substances in amphibian biological systems can give important information to illuminate contamination control measures. Coordinated effort between ecological offices, scientists, and neighborhood networks is imperative for executing successful techniques to lessen contamination releases.

Executing and upholding arrangements that limit the utilization of hurtful synthetic compounds in agribusiness, industry, and local locations can add to further developing water quality. Feasible land the executives rehearses, riparian cradle zones, and wetland protection endeavors can go about as regular channels, assisting with alleviating the effect of toxins on Normal Crackpot natural surroundings.

Environmental Change Transformation Methodologies

Given the certainty of environmental change influences, protection methodologies should likewise incorporate transformation measures to assist Normal Nut cases with adapting to the evolving climate. Checking shifts in reproducing and movement designs, grasping the accessibility of reasonable environments under changing climatic circumstances, and executing defensive measures during weak periods are essential parts of environmental change variation.

Worldwide drives to address environmental change, decrease ozone depleting substance emanations, and upgrade versatility in biological systems can have expansive advantages for Normal Nut case populaces. Partaking in peaceful accords and upholding for approaches that focus on environment activity are fundamental commitments to getting the drawn out endurance of crackpots and other weak species.

6. **Cooperative Exploration and Checking Projects**

Logical Exploration for Informed Protection

Proceeded with logical examination is crucial for grasping the complexities of Normal Nut case environment and conduct. Far reaching concentrates on their rearing science, searching propensities, relocation examples, and reactions to ecological changes give basic experiences to informed preservation techniques.

Cooperative exploration endeavors including ornithologists, environmentalists, and preservation researcher add to the group of information fundamental for creating designated protection mediations. Long haul observing projects that track populace patterns, conceptive achievement, and wellbeing markers are vital for surveying the adequacy of protection gauges and adjusting systems depending on the situation.

5.2 Poetic responses to environmental challenges and the call for conservation

Verse, with its suggestive power and capacity to mix the profundities of human inclination, has long filled in as a convincing mechanism for resolving major problems.

Notwithstanding heightening ecological difficulties, writers have arisen as expressive voices, winding around refrains that eloquent the criticalness of protection. This investigation dives into the graceful reactions to ecological difficulties, looking at how writers explore the intricacies of nature's predicament, inspire a feeling of environmental cognizance, and call for extraordinary preservation activity.

1. **Nature as Dream: The Love in Graceful Reflections**
   The Magnificent in Nature: A Wellspring of Motivation
   Nature, in the entirety of its highness and weakness, has been a perpetual dream for writers across hundreds of years. The wonderful scenes, the fragile exchange of environments, and the perplexing excellence of widely varied vegetation give a broad material to idyllic investigation. Writers draw motivation from the greatness of mountains, the serenity of lakes, and the fleeting magnificence of seasons, involving nature as a figurative mirror to mirror the human condition.
   Natural Mindfulness: A Writer's Vision
   As natural difficulties escalate, writers are progressively turning their look toward environmental mindfulness. The acknowledgment of the sensitive equilibrium inside biological systems, the delicacy of biodiversity, and the interconnectedness of all living creatures turns into a focal topic in contemporary nature verse. Writers act as observers to the evolving scenes, catching the unobtrusive subtleties of ecological changes and thinking about the significant effect of human exercises on the normal world.

2. **The Language of Misfortune: Wonderful Requiems for a Changing Earth**
   Evaporating Scenes: Mourns for the Vanishing
   Writers, sensitive to the beat of the Earth, make epitaphs for evaporating scenes. As urbanization infringes upon once-perfect regions, and as regular natural surroundings are lost to advancement, artists grieve the hopeless loss of biodiversity and the annihilation of environments. The language of misfortune saturates these refrains, communicating the despondency for vanishing vegetation and the irreversibility of environmental harm.
   Annihilation Songs of devotion: Grieving the Withdrew
   In a time set apart by sped up paces of species eradication, artists make termination songs of praise that memorialize the animals lost to the determined walk of anthropogenic exercises. These elegiac stanzas act as impactful tokens of the interconnected trap of life, encouraging perusers to face the gravity of biodiversity misfortune. Through the language of distress, writers call for aggregate reflection and activity to forestall further eradications.

3. **Ecopoetry: Exploring the Convergences of Nature and Activism**
   Ecopoetry as a Scholarly Development
   Ecopoetry arises as a particular scholarly development that wires lovely articulation with natural activism. Artists inside the ecopoetic custom draw in with the intricacies of natural difficulties, utilizing their refrains not exclusively to bring

out close to home reactions yet additionally to catalyze biological awareness. Ecopoetry rises above the limits of individual experience, welcoming perusers to consider the more extensive ramifications of humankind's relationship with the regular world.

Activism in Refrain: An Invitation to battle

Installed inside ecopoetry is an invitation to battle — a solicitation to perusers to become stewards of the Earth. Writers, as natural promoters, utilize their sections to stir a feeling of obligation and earnestness.

Whether tending to deforestation, environmental change, or contamination, these wonderful activists weave convincing accounts that beg society to perceive the unavoidable dangers to the planet and move toward protection.

4. **Envisioning Choices: Idealistic Dreams in Nature Verse**
   Idealistic Scenes: Imagining Amicability

   Because of natural difficulties, writers frequently adventure into the domain of idealistic dreams. These sections envision elective scenes where humankind coincides agreeably with nature, where environments flourish, and where the sensitive equilibrium of the Earth is reestablished. Idealistic nature verse fills in as both a study of current ecological practices and a confident investigation of what could be accomplished through preservation endeavors.

   Helpful Accounts: Wonderful Diagrams for Change

   Artists, as planners of language, develop supportive accounts that offer wonderful outlines for extraordinary change. These refrains imagine reforested skylines, restored biological systems, and recharged associations among humankind and the normal world. Through these creative builds, writers move perusers to partake in the rebuilding of the Earth, encouraging a feeling of organization and strengthening despite natural difficulties effectively.

5. **The Imagery of Seasons: Allegories for Change in Nature Verse**
   Occasional Allegories: Impressions of Change

   Artists frequently utilize the imagery of seasons as analogies for change in nature verse. The cyclicality of nature's seasons turns into an impression of the extraordinary potential innate in protection endeavors. From the resurrection of spring to the thoughtfulness of winter, artists utilize occasional illustrations to convey the repetitive idea of natural difficulties and the expectation for recharging through careful stewardship.

   The Fall and Rise: Pre-winter Reflections

   Pre-winter, with its distinctive shades and the shedding of leaves, turns into a strong illustration in nature verse. Artists utilize the symbolism of tumble to investigate the results of natural corruption, representing the deficiency of biodiversity and the blurring energy of biological systems. Nonetheless, inside the despairing of harvest time reflections, there is likewise the commitment of recharging — the seeds of trust that lie underneath fallen leaves, anticipating the right circumstances for germination.

6. **Mutual Voices: Verse as an Impetus for Aggregate Activity**
   Compilations of Concern: Joining Voices for Protection
   Wonderful reactions to ecological difficulties find reverberation in treasurys that join different voices in a chorale of concern. Ecological collections, organized by writers and activists, unite a variety of points of view, encounters, and wonderful styles. These assortments intensify the earnestness of preservation, encouraging a feeling of shared liability and rousing perusers to join the aggregate undertaking to defend the Earth.

   Verse Readings and Activism: The Verbally expressed Word as Impetus
   Verse readings, whether in actual social affairs or through computerized stages, act as strong impetuses for natural activism. Artists, through the verbally expressed word, imbue their stanzas with energy and conviction, convincing crowds to draw in with the natural subjects investigated in their work. Verse turns into a vessel for shared encounters and a source of inspiration, changing scholarly articulation into a powerful power for preservation.

7. **Beyond anything that can be put into words: Coordinated efforts Among Science and Verse**

Interdisciplinary Discoursed: Spanning Science and Verse

In a period where science assumes a vital part in understanding and tending to ecological difficulties, writers team up with researchers to make interdisciplinary exchanges. These coordinated efforts overcome any issues between exact information and creative articulation, encouraging a more profound comprehension of natural complexities. Researchers contribute information and bits of knowledge, while writers imbue their refrains with the close to home and tasteful elements of ecological issues, making an all encompassing story that resounds with a wide crowd.

Natural Humanities: Verse as a Problem solver

Inside the domain of natural humanities, verse arises as a problem solver. This interdisciplinary field perceives the interconnectedness of human culture, reasoning, and the climate. Artists add to ecological humanities by offering nuanced viewpoints on the moral and profound components of preservation. Through this mix of creative and scholarly disciplines, verse turns into an impetus for groundbreaking reasoning and activity.

5.3 The role of poetry in raising awareness about the conservation of the loon and its habitat

In the sensitive biological systems of lakes and streams, where the unpleasant calls of the Normal Nut case mesh into the texture of nature, verse arises as a strong device for bringing issues to light about the pressing requirement for preservation.

The job of verse rises above simple words; it turns into a vessel for profound reverberation, an impetus for understanding, and a source of inspiration in protecting the nut case and its natural surroundings.

1. **Catching the Embodiment: The Artist as Nature's Mediator**
   Writers, likened to naturalists of language, have a special capacity to catch the substance of the crackpot and its territory. Through distinctive symbolism, musical rhythm, and painstakingly picked words, writers paint representations of lakeshores enhanced with lily cushions, mirroring the nut case's outline against the brilliant shades of a sunset. They articulate the quietness of twilight waters upset simply by the cadenced jumps of nut cases looking for food. In these idyllic materials, the nut case turns out to be in excess of a bird; it changes into an image of the flawless excellence that requires our security.

2. **Reverberations of Natural Amicability: Verse as Preservation Song of praise**
   Verse fills in as a song of praise for natural concordance, winding around refrains that reverberate with the interconnectedness of the nut case and its living space. Writers dig into the advantageous connections between the nut case, the oceanic vegetation, and the fragile equilibrium of the environment. Through analogy and moral story, they articulate the significant manners by which upsetting one component can resound through the whole biological orchestra. These idyllic stories become a clarion call, encouraging perusers to perceive the delicacy of this congruity and to participate in preservation endeavors effectively.

3. **The Language of Misfortune: Idyllic Requiems for Disappearing Living spaces**
   As lakeshores capitulate to improvement and the once-perfect environments of the nut case evaporate, writers create epitaphs for these vanishing scenes. The language of misfortune penetrates these sections, communicating misery for the irreversible adjustments to the nut case's normal home. Artists grieve the infringement of substantial designs upon the quiet favorable places, the disturbance of settling locales, and the decreasing spreads of untamed water crucial for the nut case's searching. Through elegiac refrains, verse turns into a vessel for grieving the deficiency of biodiversity and a request for protection measures.

4. **Backing in Section: The Artist as Ecological Lobbyist**
   Installed inside the lines of nut case themed verse is an inconspicuous yet strong backing for preservation. Writers arise as ecological activists, utilizing their sections to explain the impending dangers looked by the nut case and its natural surroundings. Through painstakingly made language, artists shed light on the outcomes of territory misfortune, water contamination, and human aggravations.
   They call for capable land the executives, maintainable advancement rehearses, and the conservation of regular spaces critical for the crackpot's endurance. In this job, writers become heroes of the crackpot's objective, overcoming any issues between imaginative articulation and ecological activism.

5. **Rousing Association: Beautiful Solicitations to Preservation Activity**
   The reminiscent force of verse lies in its capacity to move a profound close to home association with the normal world. Writers welcome perusers to

manufacture a special interaction with the crackpot and its territory through the magnificence of language. By submerging perusers in the tactile extravagance of lakeside scenes, the writers fuel a feeling of stewardship and obligation. Perusers, dazzled by the expressive portrayals of the nut case's way of behaving and its importance in the biological system, are provoked to move toward protection.

6. **Imagining Conceivable outcomes: Idealistic Dreams in Nut case Themed Verse**

   Artists, in their creative ability, imagine idealistic scenes where the crackpot flourishes in undisturbed environments. Through sections that portray reestablished lakeshores, flourishing environments, and an agreeable concurrence among mankind and nature, writers offer looks at what could be accomplished through committed preservation endeavors. These idealistic dreams act as idyllic plans, moving perusers to imagine and effectively pursue a future where the crackpot's territory is secured and safeguarded.

7. **Joint effort with Science: Lovely Discoursed for Preservation**

In the interdisciplinary field of preservation, writers work together with researchers, making discoursed that mix creative articulation with observational information. These coordinated efforts improve the account around crackpot protection by incorporating logical bits of knowledge into beautiful refrains. The marriage of logical information with the close to home reverberation of verse makes a strong story that addresses both the mind and the heart, encouraging a more significant comprehension of the difficulties looked by the nut case and the environments it possesses.

Chapter 6

Notable Poets and Their Works

Verse, as a fine art, has been a vehicle for significant articulation, exemplifying the human involvement with words that reverberate across time and culture. Through the ages, certain writers have arisen as signals of artistic brightness, their works drawing permanent imprints on the texture of language and creative mind. This investigation takes you on an excursion through the lives and works of eminent writers, crossing different times, kinds, and social scenes.

1. **Old Voices Resounding Through Time**
1. **Homer (c. eighth Century BCE - c. eighth Century BCE)**
   Homer, a puzzling figure of old Greece, is credited with the legendary sonnets "The Iliad" and "The Odyssey." These stupendous works dig into the brave endeavors of characters like Achilles and Odysseus, investigating topics of honor, destiny, and the human condition. Homer's account ability and graceful language established the groundwork for traditional writing and have propelled innumerable essayists as the centuries progressed.

   II. Traditional Tastefulness: The Verse of Ancient times
2. **Sappho (c. 630 - c. 570 BCE)**
   Sappho, the verse writer of antiquated Greece, created refrains that praised love, magnificence, and the intricacies of the human heart. However a lot of her work is lost to time, sections of her verse known as "Sapphic refrains" persevere, uncovering a significant aversion to feeling and an investigation of want. Sappho's impact on the verse custom resounds underway of artists across societies.

3. **Virgil (70 BCE - 19 BCE)**
   Virgil, the Roman writer, created the amazing sonnet "The Aeneid," an awe-inspiring that follows the legend Aeneas as he escapes the fall of Troy and turns into the progenitor of Rome. Virgil's work magnified the greatness of Rome as well as investigated the intricacies of destiny, obligation, and the expense of

domain. "The Aeneid" remains as a demonstration of Virgil's dominance of the legendary structure.

III. The Medieval times: Supernatural Dreams and Dignified Love

4. **Dante Alighieri (1265 - 1321)**

Dante, the Italian writer, wrote "The Heavenly Satire," a figurative excursion through a lot of hardship, Limbo, and Heaven. This legendary work is a significant investigation of religious philosophy, ethical quality, and the human spirit. Dante's utilization of the vernacular Italian language raised it to a scholarly power, forming the course of Italian writing and impacting writers around the world.

5. **Geoffrey Chaucer (c. 1343 - 1400)**

Chaucer, frequently hailed as the "Father of English Writing," expressed "The Canterbury Stories." This show-stopper is an assortment of stories told by explorers en route to Canterbury, offering a clear scene of middle age English society. Chaucer's imaginative utilization of vernacular English denoted a urgent second in the development of the English language.

IV. The Renaissance: A Thriving of Creative Articulation

6. **William Shakespeare (1564 - 1616)**

Shakespeare, the Troubadour of Avon, needs no presentation. His poems and plays, for example, "Hamlet," "Romeo and Juliet," and "Macbeth," have made a permanent imprint on world writing. Shakespeare's phonetic aptitude, investigation of human brain research, and general subjects keep on reverberating, making him a persevering through figure in the scholarly group.

7. **John Milton (1608 - 1674)**

Milton, a transcending figure of English writing, created the incredible sonnet "Heaven Lost." This masterpiece dives into the scriptural story of the Fall of Man, investigating subjects of through and through freedom, defiance, and the idea of good and fiendishness. Milton's persuasiveness and philosophical profundity got his place as one of the chief artists of the English language.

V. The Heartfelt Time: Nature, Feeling, and Upheaval

8. **William Wordsworth (1770 - 1850)**

Wordsworth, a vital figure in the Heartfelt development, commended the magnificence of nature and the effortlessness of regular daily existence in sonnets like "Lines Formed a Couple of Miles Above Tintern Nunnery." His accentuation on close to home articulation and the magnificent significantly affected the direction of English verse.

9. **John Keats (1795 - 1821)**

Keats, one more light of Sentimentalism, gifted the world with flawless tributes like "Tribute to a Songbird" and "Tribute to a Grecian Urn." His expressive craftsmanship, investigation of erotic magnificence, and impactful reflections on mortality have cemented his status as one of the best writers of his age.

VI. The Victorian Age: Progress and Social Study

10. **Alfred Ruler Tennyson (1809 - 1892)**
Tennyson, the Writer Laureate of the Assembled Realm during a lot of Sovereign Victoria's rule, created sonnets that encapsulated his age. Works like "The Woman of Shalott" and "Ulysses" investigate subjects of gallantry, the effect of industrialization, and the human mission for significance.

11. **Robert Sautéing (1812 - 1889)**
Sautéing, known for his sensational discourses, dove into the complexities of the human mind. "My Last Duchess" and "The Pied Flautist of Hamelin" exhibit his story expertise and mental understanding, making him a particular voice in Victorian verse.

VII. The twentieth Hundred years: Innovation, War, and Voices of Contradiction

12. **T.S. Eliot (1888 - 1965)**
Eliot, a main figure of Pioneer verse, composed "The Waste Land," a milestone work that wrestles with the disappointment and fracture of post-The Second Great War society. His creative utilization of structure and language upset graceful articulation, making a permanent imprint on twentieth century writing.

13. **Langston Hughes (1902 - 1967)**
Hughes, a focal figure of the Harlem Renaissance, injected his verse with the rhythms and articulations of African American culture. Works like "The Negro Discusses Waterways" and "Harlem" catch the energy, difficulties, and desires of the Dark involvement with America.

VIII. Contemporary Voices: Variety, Development, and Worldwide Viewpoints

14. **Sylvia Plath (1932 - 1963)**
Plath's confession booth verse, exemplified in "Ariel" and "Woman Lazarus," investigates subjects of character, psychological maladjustment, and female experience. Her crude and extreme refrains have made her an image of scholarly trustworthiness and a critical effect on ensuing ages of writers.

15. **Seamus Heaney (1939 - 2013)**
Heaney, a Nobel laureate, investigated subjects of Irish personality, legislative issues, and the regular world in works like "Passing of a Naturalist" and "The Fix at Troy." His rich symbolism and nuanced reflections on history and struggle add to the complex embroidery of contemporary verse.

16. **Mary Oliver (1935 - 2019)**
Oliver's verse, well established in the normal world, welcomes perusers to consider the magnificence and interconnectedness of life. Works like "Wild Geese" and "The Mid year Day" commend the straightforwardness of presence and the significant illustrations nature gives.

17. **Derek Walcott (1930 - 2017)**

Walcott, a Nobel laureate, investigated the intricacies of Caribbean personality and post-imperialism in sonnets like "Omeros" and "The Ocean is History." His utilization of language and commitment with social subjects feature the worldwide reach of contemporary verse.

This brief look into the lives and works of striking writers traverses hundreds of years and landmasses, featuring the variety, advancement, and persevering through effect of beautiful articulation. From old sagas to contemporary voices, every artist adds to the rich embroidery of human experience, making a permanent imprint on the always developing scene of writing.

6.1 Analysis of poems by well-known poets featuring the Common Loon

Verse, with its capacity to rise above the bounds of language and catch the pith of the human experience, has frequently turned its look to the normal world. Among the heap animals that have propelled writers, the Normal Nut case remains as an image of wild, tormenting lakeshores with its spooky calls and dazzling the creative mind of essayists. This investigation digs into sonnets by notable artists that highlight the Normal Nut case, dissecting how these refrains enlighten the bird's persona, investigate its environment, and represent more extensive topics inside the domain of nature and human life.

1. **Robert Ice: "The Broiler Bird"**
   In the tremendous collection of Robert Ice's work, "The Broiler Bird" stands apart as a sonnet that unpretentiously consolidates the presence of the Normal Nut case. While the essential spotlight is on the Stove Bird, known for its dreary melody, Ice winds in references to the crackpot, making a layered investigation of nature's soundscape.

   The sonnet starts with the perception of the Stove Bird's tune, portrayed as "unctuous A fluid that will convey." As the sections unfurl, Ice presents the crackpot with the line "The solstice still incrimsoned on the ocean." Here, the reference to the solstice lines up with the nut case's presence, as they are frequently connected with northern lakes and summer rearing seasons.

   Ice's decision of "incrimsoned" adds a nuanced layer, recommending the crackpot's frightful call as a ruby stained reverberation on the waters. The symbolism summons both the excellence and the despairing of the crackpot's cry, interfacing it to the more extensive subject of nature's persevering cycles and the progression of time.

   The juxtaposition of the Broiler Bird and the crackpot makes an ensemble of sounds inside the sonnet, mirroring the variety and intricacy of nature's voices. Ice, a sharp onlooker of the regular world, utilizes the crackpot to enhance the hear-able scene of the sonnet, welcoming perusers to ponder the interconnectedness of avian songs in nature.

2. **Alden Nowlan: "Loonie"**
   Alden Nowlan, a Canadian writer known for his sharp bits of knowledge into

country life and the normal world, presents the Normal Crackpot in a strong and intelligent light in his sonnet "Loonie." The actual title, with its conversational reference to the Canadian one-dollar coin highlighting a nut case, establishes the vibe for a more profound investigation.

Nowlan's sonnet ponders the frightful cry of the nut case and its representative reverberation. The initial lines quickly cause to notice the bird's vocalization: "The loonie has a moaning cry/that penetrates the vacancy of the sky." Here, the nut case's cry turns into a sonic image, slicing through the boundlessness of the sky and repeating a feeling of isolation.

As the sonnet advances, Nowlan digs into the representative layers related with the crackpot. The loonie, past its avian namesake, turns into a similitude for the writer's own existential reflections. Nowlan ponders the repeating idea of life, typified in the picture of the "wheeling gulls," and recommends that the crackpot's cry conveys the heaviness of aggregate memory.

The sonnet's end lines stress the extraordinary nature of the crackpot's cry: "It goes up,/and up,/till you can't hear it/any more." This rising mirrors the artist's thought of life's direction, the climb into the obscure, and a definitive quietness that follows. Nowlan's "Loonie" consequently turns into a reflection on the transient magnificence of life, embodied in the eerie call of the nut case.

3. **Mary Oliver: "The Nut case"**

Mary Oliver, celebrated for her significant association with the normal world, brings her unmistakable style to the depiction of the Normal Nut case in her sonnet basically named "The Crackpot." In this piece, Oliver catches the bird's persona and evokes thought on the sensitive harmony among nature and the human spectator.

The sonnet opens with an immediate location to the crackpot, laying out a prompt feeling of association: "Not exactly a tune, not exactly a whistle,/it was more the ascent and fall of a word,/a word that before long took off." Oliver's decision of language is significant; she portrays the nut case's call as a semantic articulation, outlining it as a type of correspondence that rises above the human limit with regards to language.

Oliver then investigates the duality of the crackpot's presence, both in the physical and otherworldly domains. The crackpot's call, portrayed as "two horns," proposes a double - maybe life and passing, presence and nonattendance. This dualism lines up with Oliver's more extensive topical investigation of the interconnectedness of every living being.

The writer welcomes perusers to participate in the demonstration of seeing the crackpot's call: "and you, feeling briefly/like you could enter them —/both the voice, and the world." This snapshot of closeness highlights Oliver's way of thinking of direct commitment with nature, empowering perusers to understand the nut case and, likewise, the regular world.

In the closing lines, Oliver thinks about the transient idea of the crackpot's presence, both in the physical and hear-able domains. The crackpot's call, compared to "a wheeling linguistic structure," turns into a similitude for the repeating idea of presence. Oliver's "The Crackpot" is a demonstration of her capacity to distil significant experiences from the easiest minutes in nature, welcoming perusers to take part in a pensive exchange with their general surroundings.

4. **Wendell Berry: "The Tranquility of Wild Things"**

While not expressly highlighting the Normal Nut case, Wendell Berry's sonnet "The Tranquility of Wild Things" catches the quintessence of the crackpot's environment and the serenity related with the regular world. Berry, a writer, rancher, and ecological dissident, investigates the helpful force of nature, making a thoughtful space that reverberates with the tranquility frequently connected with crackpot possessed lakes.

sonnet starts with an admission of the writer's battle with human tensions: "When despair for the world fills in me/and I wake in the night basically sound/ in feeling of dread toward what my life and my youngsters' lives might be." Berry recognizes the heaviness of contemporary difficulties, repeating the worries of many living in a quickly impacting world.

Be that as it may, the sonnet takes an extraordinary turn as Berry looks for comfort in nature: "I proceed to rests where the wood drake/rests in his magnificence on the water, and the incredible heron takes care of." Here, the writer submerges himself in the normal world, tracking down shelter in the organization of wild animals. While the particular notice of the nut case is missing, the summoning of waterfowl and their serene presence resounds with the mood of crackpot occupied lakeshores.

Berry's decision of the expression "the tranquility of wild things" epitomizes the focal subject of the sonnet. The writer tracks down comfort in the wild, where "the presence of still water" turns into an illustration for the quieting impact of nature. This intelligent respite amidst the normal world differentiations with the tensions of human life, offering a strong critique on the mending force of the climate.

5. **E. B. Yet again white: "to the Lake"**

E. B. Yet again white's exposition "to the Lake" is a takeoff from regular verse, yet it embodies a nuanced investigation of the human instinct relationship, reverberating with subjects present in nut case driven verse. White's exposition ponders his re-visitation of a lake where he spent summers as a youngster, and the suggestive story catches the immortal embodiment of normal scenes.

White's perceptions, as he returns to the lake, reverberation the tactile extravagance frequently connected with nut case environments. He portrays the "weak mix of the breeze," the "sound of the speedboats," and the "lapping of the lake water." While crackpots aren't unequivocally referenced, the setting lines up with the quiet lakeshores frequently preferred by these notable birds.

The exposition takes a pensive turn as White ponders the repeating idea of life and the interconnectedness of ages. He notices his child participating in exercises suggestive of his own experience growing up, obscuring the fleeting limits among over a significant time span. This worldly progression reflects the recurrent examples saw in nature, resounding with the subjects present in crackpot themed verse.

White's work fills in as a composition partner to nut case motivated verse, offering a story investigation of the profound associations between memory, nature, and the progression of time. The ageless nature of lake scenes, as portrayed by White, lines up with the getting through persona of the Normal Crackpot's living space.

6. **Examination and Subjects Across Sonnets**

1. **Nature's Sonic Scene**

In these sonnets, the Normal Crackpot arises as a focal figure in nature's sonic scene. The unpleasant calls of the nut case, portrayed as moaning, repeating, or rising and falling, become emblematic strings winding through the refrains.

This hear-able presence makes a feeling of quickness, welcoming perusers to draw in with the crackpot's vocalizations as a particular component of the normal world.

2. **Imagery and Analogy**

The nut case, past its avian presence, takes on emblematic importance in these sonnets. It turns into a representation for existential reflections, the transient excellence of life, and the interconnectedness of every living being. The crackpot's cry, with its dualism and repeating nature, fills in as a piercing image that resounds past the bounds of avian imagery, improving the topical layers of the verse.

3. **Human instinct Association**

Across these sonnets, there is an ongoing idea of the human instinct association. Writers address the crackpot not just as an outer subject however as a piece of a common biological system. The demonstration of seeing the nut case's presence turns into a method for going into a more profound comprehension of the normal world, cultivating compassion, and welcoming perusers to ponder their place inside this multifaceted snare of life.

4. **Fleeting Congruity and Cycles**

The topic of transient congruity and cycles is predominant in the investigation of the Normal Nut case. Whether it's Ice's appearance on the solstice, Nowlan's examination of life's wheeling gulls, or Oliver's thought of the wheeling linguistic structure of the nut case's cry, there is an acknowledgment of life's repeating nature. The crackpot turns into a standard for examining the progression of time, the certainty of progress, and the getting through cycles inside the normal world.

5. **Isolation and Serenity**

A large number of these sonnets inspire a feeling of isolation and serenity related with the nut case's environment. The tranquil lakeshores, the ascent and fall of the crackpot's cry, and the intelligent stops in nature welcome perusers to track down comfort in nature. This subject lines up with more extensive reflections on the helpful force of nature and its capacity to offer a relief from the tensions of human life.

6. **Pensive Commitment with Nature**

These writers welcome perusers into a scrutinizing commitment with nature, encouraging them to go past simple perception and drench themselves in the sights, sounds, and representative reverberation of the crackpot. The demonstration of seeing the nut case turns into a channel for contemplation, a method for interfacing with the secrets of the regular world, and an encouragement to manufacture a more profound relationship with the climate.

6.2 Exploration of different styles and perspectives in loon-themed poetry

The domain of crackpot themed verse is a tremendous and changed scene, similar as the lakeshores the Normal Nut case calls home. Writers, spellbound by the persona of this famous bird, have utilized different styles and viewpoints to express their perceptions, feelings, and reflections. This investigation dives into the rich woven artwork of nut case themed verse, disentangling the particular styles and viewpoints that writers bring to this avian dream.

1. **Customary Structures: Reverberations of Elegance**
1. **Work Groupings**
   In the practice of traditional verse, a few journalists have created piece groupings committed to the Normal Crackpot. The organized idea of pieces, with their severe rhyme plans and meter, offers writers a restrained material to investigate the subtleties of the nut case's presence. Inside the fourteen lines, artists can convey the bird's ethereal calls, the excellence of its plumage, and the despairing of its environment.
2. **Haiku and Tanka**

Drawing motivation from Japanese idyllic structures, haiku and tanka carry curtness and accuracy to crackpot themed sections. In the moderate design of haiku, writers distil the quintessence of crackpot experiences into three lines, frequently zeroing in on a solitary second or normal component. Tanka, with its drawn out structure, takes into consideration a more extensive investigation, empowering writers to bring out the environment of lakeshores and the subtle charm of the nut case.

II. **Free Refrain: Releasing Expressive Opportunity**

1. **Walt Whitmanesque Festivals**
   In the soul of Walt Whitman's extensive and celebratory style, a few writers

utilize free refrain to sing the gestures of recognition of the Normal Crackpot. This approach embraces the opportunity to investigate differed rhythms, line lengths, and linguistic designs. Through free section, writers catch the powerful energy of the nut case in flight, the musical rhythm of its calls, and the interconnectedness of nature with a Whitmanesque extravagance.

2. **Inadequate Imagism**

Alternately, different writers embrace a scanty and imagistic free stanza style to distil nut case experiences to their embodiment. Via cautiously choosing clear and reminiscent symbolism, these writers make depictions of lakeshores, accentuating the moderate magnificence of the nut case's natural surroundings.

This style frequently welcomes perusers to connect effectively with the stanzas, occupying the spaces between pictures with their own tactile encounters.

III. Confession booth and Individual Points of view: The Writer as Eyewitness

1. **Confession booth Reflections**
   In the confession booth style, artists mix nut case themed stanzas with individual reflections and encounters. The crackpot turns into a mirror mirroring the writer's feelings, recollections, and existential insights. This approach welcomes perusers into a close exchange with the writer's internal scene, investigating how the crackpot fills in as a vessel for self-revelation and reflection.

2. **Nature as a Representation for Oneself**

Expanding on the confession booth approach, a few writers utilize the crackpot as a similitude for oneself. In these sections, the bird's way of behaving, calls, and territory become emblematic impressions of the writer's internal world. This figurative interaction adds layers of significance to nut case themed verse, changing the avian subject into a flexible and resounding image.

IV. Account Investigations: Narrating with the Nut case as Hero

1. **Environmental Stories**
   Writers frequently take on a story style to investigate the biological elements of the crackpot's territory. Through narrating, they weave multifaceted stories of lakeshores overflowing with life, the difficulties looked by the crackpot, and the fragile equilibrium of biological systems. This approach connects with perusers in a more extensive story about ecological protection and the interconnected snare of life encompassing the Normal Crackpot.

2. **Authentic Narrating**

A few writers dive into verifiable narrating, securing nut case themed refrains with regards to human connections with the bird over the long run. Whether investigating native legend, fables, or the effect of human exercises on the crackpot's environment, these story investigations give a verifiable focal point through which perusers can examine the changing elements among mankind and the nut case.

V. Exploratory Methodologies: Pushing Limits

1. **Coordinated efforts with Visual Expressions**
   In the domain of exploratory verse, a few essayists team up with visual specialists to make media encounters. The combination of nut case themed stanzas with visual components like canvases, photos, or computerized media adds another layer of tangible wealth. This interdisciplinary methodology welcomes perusers to draw in with crackpot themed verse as a multisensory and vivid experience.
2. **Soundscapes and Sound Verse**

Going past the composed word, writers explore different avenues regarding sound verse to catch the hear-able scene of the nut case. Through recorded readings, surrounding sounds, and in any event, consolidating genuine nut case calls, these artists make sonic encounters that transport audience members to the lakeshores where the Normal Crackpot holds influence. This imaginative methodology blends verse with the instinctive effect of sound, cultivating a more profound association with the avian subject.

VI. Multifaceted Investigations: Worldwide Viewpoints on the Crackpot

1. **Social Imagery**
   The Normal Crackpot holds social importance in different locales, and artists from assorted foundations investigate the bird's imagery in their social setting. Whether as a tribal figure, an image of wild, or an animal implanted in fables, these sonnets give a diverse focal point through which perusers can see the value in the multi-layered imagery of the crackpot.
2. **Bilingual and Multilingual Articulations**

In nut case themed verse, bilingual and multilingual articulations advance the phonetic scene. Writers weave sections in numerous dialects, mirroring the phonetic variety of locales where the crackpot is a conspicuous figure. This approach celebrates etymological wealth as well as adds layers of social reverberation to the investigation of the Normal Nut case.

6.3 The evolution of loon poetry over time

The rich embroidery of crackpot verse unfurls like the first light over a serene lake, its strings woven through hundreds of years of human reflection and articulation. The Normal Nut case, with its unpleasant calls and puzzling presence, has roused writers across time and societies. This investigation follows the development of crackpot verse, unwinding the beautiful excursion from antiquated reverberations to present day dreams.

1. **Old and Old style Reverberations: Mythic Crackpots in Section**
1. **Antiquated Imagery**
   In the chronicles of old verse, crackpots arise as images weighed down with mythic importance. From old Greek and Roman writers to the stanzas of Chinese and Local American minstrels, the crackpot turns into an animal of social imagery. In these early sonnets, the crackpot frequently represents secret, progress, and the liminal spaces between universes.
2. **Sapphic Murmurs and Traditional Reverberations**

Sappho, the verse artist of old Greece, deified the crackpot's unpleasant cry in stanzas that commended love and nature. However sections of her work remain, Sappho's references to the crackpot persevere, conveying the substance of the bird's persona across centuries. The crackpot, in these old sections, turns into a lovely vehicle for communicating the unutterable and the transient idea of magnificence.

II. Middle age Thoughts: Metaphorical Trips of Extravagant

1. **Bestiaries and Emblematic Symbolism**
   During the middle age time frame, nut cases tracked down their place in bestiaries and metaphorical verse. These lovely works frequently doled out representative implications to creatures, and the crackpot, with its unmistakable way of behaving and tormenting calls, turned into a figurative dream. In the bestiaries, the crackpot's cries could represent the spirit's longing or the fleeting idea of life.
2. **Dignified Love and Nature's Mourn**

As middle age verse embraced elegant love and the sentiment of nature, the nut case took on new aspects. In the cultured love custom, the crackpot's calls may be woven into mourns, reflecting the subjects of solitary love or the despairing of partition. The bird's subtle presence on lakeshores turned into an idyllic figure of speech for the longing and disconnection experienced by darlings.

III. Renaissance Dreams: Nature's Agreement Disclosed

1. **Eclogues and Nature's Beautiful Range**
   The Renaissance introduced a restored interest in the normal world, and writers praised the magnificence of lakeshores and the animals that possessed them.
   In peaceful eclogues, the crackpot could make an appearance, its calls turning out to be important for the orchestra of nature. Writers like Edmund Spenser and Sir Philip Sidney wove crackpot roused symbolism into their refrains, depicting the bird as an agreeable component in charming scenes.

2. Imagery in Significant Verse

In significant verse of the Renaissance, where visual images went with sections, the crackpot may be portrayed as a token of isolation or secret. These emblematic portrayals offered a visual supplement to the idyllic investigation of the bird's importance, making a multi-tactile encounter for perusers.

IV. Heartfelt Reverberation: The Eminent and the Lone

1. **Wordsworthian Examinations**
   The Heartfelt time, with its accentuation on nature's magnificent and the singular's association with the normal world, gave a ripe ground to crackpot roused verse. William Wordsworth, a conspicuous figure of Sentimentalism, pondered the magnificence of nature in his stanzas. While not expressly highlighting the crackpot, Wordsworth's emphasis on the superb and the single reverberates with the feeling of nut case occupied lakeshores.
2. **Keatsian Erotic nature**

John Keats, one more illuminating presence of the Heartfelt development, investigated sexy excellence and mortality in his tributes. While the crackpot probably won't have been an immediate subject, Keats' melodious craftsmanship and commitment with the fleeting idea of presence line up with the topics frequently connected with the nut case in later verse.

V. Victorian Varieties: Ornithological Tributes and Preservationist Concerns

1. **Tennysonian Love**
   The Victorian period saw an interest with ornithology, and Alfred Ruler Tennyson, the Writer Laureate of the Unified Realm, communicated this in refrains celebrating birds. While not explicitly including the nut case, Tennyson's ornithological tributes catch the Victorian interest with avian life, laying the basis for later artists to dig into additional particular investigations of the crackpot.
2. **Carmelizing's Mental Representations**
   Robert Carmelizing, known for his sensational speeches, might have offered mental representations including the nut case as a person. While there is no immediate proof of nut case themed discourses, Cooking's account ability and mental understanding set up for artists to dive into the intricacies of the crackpot's presence in later years.
3. **Early Protection Concerns**

Towards the conclusion of the Victorian age, early protection concerns started to arise. As industrialization infringed upon normal environments, artists could thely affect bird species, including the nut case. These unobtrusive clues in Victorian verse set up for additional express natural appearance in later years.

VI. Present day Reflections: Natural Hymns and Contemplative Investigations

1. **Mid-twentieth Hundred years: Ecological Arousing**
   The mid-twentieth century denoted a defining moment in ecological mindfulness, and writers started to wrestle with the effect of human exercises on the normal world. While the Normal Nut case probably won't have been the essential concentration, sonnets from this period frequently conveyed natural undercurrents, tending to the sensitive harmony among mankind and the climate.

2. **Late twentieth Hundred years: Nut cases as Images of Wild**
   As natural developments picked up speed, the nut case arose as an image of wild and protection. Artists, especially those with associations with districts occupied by nut cases, started to make stanzas that praised the bird's strength and pointed out the requirement for ecological stewardship.

3. **21st Hundred years: Diverse Points of view**

In the 21st hundred years, nut case verse has embraced a bunch of points of view. Writers draw from natural experiences, individual reflections, and a worldwide cognizance of ecological difficulties. The Normal Nut case, when a figure of old legends and Victorian interest, presently remains at the crossing point of social imagery, natural support, and thoughtful investigation in contemporary verse.

VII. Lovely Topics Across Periods: A Progression of Reflections

1. **The Unpleasant Call as a Theme**
   Across periods, the frightful call of the nut case perseveres as a focal theme in crackpot verse. Whether communicated through old style imagery, Heartfelt consideration, or current ecological hymns, the nut case's call stays a suggestive string that integrates hundreds of years of lovely reflections.

2. **Nature's Emblematic Reverberation**
   The emblematic reverberation of the crackpot advances with every period. From old mythic imagery to Victorian symbolic portrayals and current moderate purposeful anecdotes, the crackpot's importance rises above time. It turns into an image of isolation, secret, and, in contemporary verse, a harbinger of ecological mindfulness.

3. **Human instinct Association**
   A repetitive topic in nut case verse is the association among people and nature. Whether depicted through peaceful eclogues, Wordsworthian isolations, or contemporary ecological reflections, writers reliably investigate the complicated connection among humankind and the nut case's living space.

4. **Ecological Worries and Protection Stories**

While early protection concerns quietly showed up in Victorian verse, current and contemporary writers unequivocally mesh natural worries into their refrains. The effect of human exercises on the nut case's natural surroundings, environmental change, and the call for preservation make a story circular segment that ranges from unpretentious clues in Victorian stanzas to critical requests in 21st-century songs of devotion.

Chapter 7

Creative Writing Prompts and Exercises

Experimental writing prompts and activities act as amazing assets to light creative mind, beat an inability to write, and upgrade narrating abilities. Whether you're a hopeful essayist looking for motivation or a carefully prepared writer hoping to break out of standard, the different universe of prompts and activities offers a horde of conceivable outcomes.

The Significance of Experimental writing Prompts:

Animating Imagination:

Experimental writing prompts go about as impetuses for creative mind. They give a beginning stage, pushing scholars to investigate strange domains of their psyches and find novel thoughts.

Defeating An inability to write:

Indeed, even the most achieved authors face times of inventive dry season. Prompts offer a help during these times, filling in as an extension between the clear page and a flood of imaginative contemplations.

Enhancing Composing Styles:

Openness to various prompts urges journalists to explore different avenues regarding various kinds, tones, and styles. This variety adds to the improvement of a flexible and versatile composing range of abilities.

Sorts of Exploratory writing Prompts:

Visual Prompts:

Pictures, artistic creations, or photos can be strong prompts. They animate the visual faculties and brief scholars to make stories propelled by the subtleties inside the visual upgrades.

Word Prompts:

Single words or a mix of words can set off one of a kind thoughts. These prompts challenge essayists to investigate the subtleties of language, revealing startling associations between apparently inconsequential ideas.

Situation Prompts:

Setting the stage with a particular situation or circumstance prompts scholars to envision how characters would answer. These prompts frequently lead to the making of dynamic and connecting with stories.

Making Compelling Experimental writing Activities:

Character Improvement Activities:

Make prompts that dig into the complexities of character creation. Investigate a person's experience, inspirations, and fears, pushing scholars to fabricate balanced and engaging personas.

Setting Investigation Activities:

Urge journalists to zero in on setting as a focal component of their accounts. Whether it's a cutting edge cityscape or an interesting town, prompts that stress clear depictions improve the general lavishness of narrating.

Discourse Practice Activities:

Making true and connecting with discourse is an expertise that can be sharpened through designated works out. Use prompts that expect characters to participate in significant discussions, exploring clashes or sharing crucial minutes.

Fitting Prompts to Various Kinds:

Sci-fi and Dream Prompts:

Transport journalists to extraordinary domains with prompts that include advanced innovation, mystical domains, or extraterrestrial experiences. These prompts support the advancement of novel and vivid universes.

Secret and Thrill ride Prompts:

Challenge scholars to make emotional accounts by giving prompts that include puzzling events, perplexing wrongdoings, or startling unexpected developments. These activities sharpen the specialty of keeping perusers as eager and anxious as ever.

Sentiment and Connections Prompts:

Investigate the intricacies of human association with prompts that dig into adoration, tragedy, and the complexities of connections. These activities assist journalists with mixing close to home profundity into their narrating.

Prompts for Various Composing Configurations:

Brief tale Prompts:

Make prompts that are helpful for brief narrating. Urge essayists to foster a total story inside a restricted word count, encouraging the capacity to convey profundity in a minimized configuration.

Verse Prompts:

Verse prompts frequently center around bringing out feelings through language and symbolism. Urge scholars to try different things with various idyllic structures, styles, and subjects, cultivating inventiveness inside the limitations of refrain.

Novel-Producing Prompts:

For those setting out on clever composition, prompts can be intended to ignite thoughts for general plots, complex characters, or the improvement of multifaceted universes. These activities give an establishment to long-frame narrating.

Integrating Prompts into Composing Schedules:

Everyday Composing Prompts:

Laying out an everyday practice of day to day composing prompts develops discipline and innovativeness. In any event, devoting a brief time frame every day to answering prompts can prompt a consistent progression of thoughts.

Bunch Composing Activities:

Composing prompts can be adjusted for social scenes, encouraging cooperative inventiveness. Whether in a study hall or a composing studio, bunch practices energize different viewpoints and shared motivation.

Customizing Prompts:

Journalists can adjust prompts to line up with their one of a kind interests and inclinations. This personalization guarantees that the inventive strategy stays pleasant and reverberates with the singular essayist's style.

7.1 Encouraging readers to engage with the themes of the book through their own poetry

Drawing in with writing goes past the demonstration of perusing; it stretches out into the domain of individual translation and articulation. One convincing method for cultivating this association is by empowering perusers to investigate the subjects of a book thanks to their own verse. This develops how they might interpret the material as well as changes them from latent buyers to dynamic givers in the scholarly discourse.

Opening Imagination:

Unique interaction to Subjects:

At the point when perusers are provoked to exemplify the subjects of a book in their verse, it prompts reflection. They dive into the characters' battles, the unexpected developments', and the fundamental messages, producing a special interaction with the story.

Opportunity of Articulation:

Verse gives a novel road to imaginative articulation. Empowering perusers to decipher and communicate the subjects as would be natural for them takes into consideration a different scope of points of view. This opportunity encourages a feeling of responsibility over the story, making the perusing experience really improving.

Exploring the Creative cycle:

Figuring out Subjects:

Prior to setting out on idyllic undertakings, perusers should initially get a handle on the subjects of the book. This includes distinguishing key themes, character advancements, and general messages. A strong comprehension establishes the groundwork for a more nuanced investigation in their verse.

Extricating Feelings:

Subjects frequently inspire explicit feelings. Whether it's the victory of affection, the give up all hope of misfortune, or the flexibility in affliction, perusers can channel these feelings into their verse. This cycle sets their association with the book as well as takes into consideration a more emotive and credible articulation.

The Job of Book Clubs and Conversations:

Making Cooperative Spaces:

Book clubs and conversation gatherings give a superb stage to perusers to share their beautiful understandings. These cooperative spaces become prolific ground for the trading of thoughts, rousing people to investigate subjects by and large and draw motivation according to assorted viewpoints.

Input and Reflection:

In such gatherings, perusers can get criticism on their verse and take part in intelligent conversations. This intuitive interaction refines their idyllic abilities as well as improves their appreciation of the book's subjects through the changed focal points of individual perusers.

Working with Studios and Occasions:

Verse Composing Studios:

Sorting out studios devoted to making an interpretation of book subjects into verse can be monstrously advantageous. Master facilitators can direct members through the cycle, offering methods to catch the substance of subjects and empowering a unique trade of thoughts.

Artistic Occasions:

Integrating verse into scholarly occasions revolved around a specific book makes a feeling of festivity. Perusers can discuss their sonnets, encouraging a public encounter that reinforces the connection between the scholarly work and its crowd.

Saddling Innovation:

Advanced Stages and Difficulties:

In the advanced age, different stages can be utilized to urge perusers to share their verse. Facilitating on the web difficulties where members submit sonnets motivated by unambiguous subjects advances boundless commitment and considers a worldwide local area of perusers to interface.

Intelligent Applications and Stages:

Creative applications and stages can give intelligent encounters, permitting perusers to draw in with subjects progressively. These stages could offer prompts, coordinated efforts, or even interactive media elements to improve the idyllic investigation of book subjects.

Advantages of Drawing in with Subjects Through Verse:

More profound Artistic Appreciation:

The demonstration of making an interpretation of subjects into verse extends perusers' appreciation for the scholarly subtleties of a book. It urges them to analyze similitudes, dissect imagery, and unravel the creator's aim, prompting a more significant comprehension of the work.

Building a Scholarly People group:

Verse propelled by book topics cultivates a feeling of local area among perusers. Shared encounters and understandings make bonds that reach out past the pages of the book, changing the demonstration of adding something extra to a cooperative and common undertaking.

Contextual analyses and Examples of overcoming adversity:

Local area Effect:

Various examples feature the positive effect of empowering perusers to communicate their understandings through verse. From nearby book clubs to online networks, perusers have tracked down comfort, motivation, and a feeling of having a place through the common experience of idyllic articulation.

Writer Peruser Association:

Creators themselves have embraced this intuitive methodology. Some have started verse challenges attached to their books, cultivating an immediate association with their perusers. This not just lifts the peruser's part in the scholarly discussion yet additionally gives creators novel experiences into the effect of their work.

7.2 Writing exercises inspired by the Common Loon and its natural environment

The Normal Crackpot, a glorious bird frequently tracked down in North American lakes, fills in as a wonderful dream for investigating the domains of experimental writing. Its unpleasant calls across quiet waters, its elegant plunges, and its interconnectedness with its normal territory offer an abundance of motivation for composing works out. In this aide, we'll dive into different activities that draw from the rich woven artwork of the Normal Nut case's current circumstance, empowering authors to drench themselves in the excellence and secret of this avian world.

Figuring out the Normal Nut case:

Observational Composition:

Start by noticing Normal Nut cases right at home. Observe their developments, the examples of their calls, and their cooperations with the climate. Make nitty gritty perceptions, leveling up the ability of catching perplexing subtleties that reinvigorate your composition.

Examination and Truth Fiction Combination:

Dive into the normal history of Normal Nut cases. Integrate real data into your composition, mixing it flawlessly with creative components. Make an account that winds around the logical comprehension of the bird with your remarkable narrating voice.

Associating with Nature:

Tangible Inundation:

Drench yourself in the regular habitat that the Normal Crackpot possesses. Shut your eyes and spotlight on the hints of water lapping against the shore, the stirring of leaves, and the far off calls of the nut cases. Utilize these tactile encounters to make clear settings in your composition.

Nature Journaling:

Keep a nature diary devoted to your experiences with the Normal Nut case. Archive your contemplations, sentiments, and perceptions. Utilize this diary as a springboard for wonderful reflections, character outlines, or even as a vault for future story thoughts.

Investigating Topics Motivated by the Normal Nut case:

Imagery and Analogy:

Investigate the imagery related with the Normal Nut case. It is many times seen as an image of wild and isolation. Make practices where journalists utilize the crackpot as a representation for different subjects like opportunity, detachment, or the sensitive equilibrium of biological systems.

Relocation and Change:

Think about the transient examples of Normal Nut cases. Utilize this regular peculiarity as an illustration for individual or cultural change. Foster composing prompts that empower reflection on the subject of change and variation.

Character Advancement:

Human Investigation:

Challenge authors to represent Normal Nut cases. Make characters that encapsulate the soul of these birds, investigating their exceptional characters, difficulties, and connections. This exercise encourages inventiveness by blending the avian and human universes.

Crackpot Roused Folklore:

Construct a folklore around Normal Crackpots. Foster activities where authors make histories, legends, or fantasies roused by the bird's qualities. This invigorates inventiveness as well as digs into social narrating customs.

Exploratory writing Prompts:

Visual Prompts:

Give pictures of Normal Nut cases in different settings. Urge authors to create brief tales, sonnets, or graphic sections enlivened by the obvious signals. The objective is to bring out the pith of the bird's reality through composed articulation.

Word Prompts:

Offer a rundown of words related with the Normal Nut case and its natural surroundings. Journalists can then involve these words as prompts to make suggestive pieces, investigating the profound and tangible components of the climate.

Exchanges and Calls:

Center around the particular calls of the Normal Crackpot. Foster activities where authors make discoursed or discussions roused by these calls. This prompts investigation of correspondence, language, and the interconnectedness of nature.

Investigating Natural Topics:

Environment Accounts:

Extend past the Normal Nut case to investigate the more extensive environment it possesses. Foster composing practices that accentuate the interconnectedness of species, the sensitive equilibrium of biological systems, and the effect of human connection.

Ecological Promotion:

Challenge essayists to involve their words as a device for ecological promotion. Foster prompts that urge them to bring issues to light about protection issues connected with the Normal Crackpot's environment. This could appear as expositions, articles, or even fictitious stories with a preservation message.

Class Explicit Activities:

Secret and Anticipation:

Create secret prompts based on the Normal Crackpot. Foster situations where the bird's ways of behaving become key to the plot, cultivating a feeling of interest and tension.

Verse Roused by Flight:

Investigate the subject of trip in nut case propelled verse. Utilize the taking off developments of the bird as an illustration for freedom, escape, or the quest for dreams. Urge writers to explore different avenues regarding musicality and symbolism propelled by the crackpot's smooth flight.

Verifiable Fiction:

Set composing practices in various verifiable periods, investigating what the presence of Normal Nut cases could have meant for human social orders or societies. This verifiable focal point adds a layer of profundity to narrating.

Studios and Cooperative Undertakings:

Composing Retreats:

Arrange composing withdraws where Normal Crackpots are predominant. These vivid encounters permit essayists to draw motivation straightforwardly from the bird's living space, encouraging a more profound association with nature and their inventive work.

Cooperative Activities:

Start cooperative tasks where journalists and visual specialists cooperate to make a multidisciplinary investigation of Normal Crackpots. Matching composed pieces with visual portrayals upgrades the general effect and gives a comprehensive creative encounter.

Computerized Stages for Sharing:

Virtual Entertainment Difficulties:

Influence virtual entertainment stages to make difficulties where scholars share their Normal Crackpot enlivened works. This not just forms a local area of similar people yet in addition energizes different understandings and articulations.

Online Discussions and Websites:

Lay out internet based gatherings or websites devoted to Normal Nut case propelled composition. Urge essayists to share their encounters, pieces, and experiences. This virtual space turns into a center for scholarly investigation and local area building.

Reflection and Correction:

Peer Survey and Input:

Integrate peer survey meetings where journalists can share their Normal Crackpot roused works. Valuable input refines their composition, cultivating a culture of non-stop improvement.

Intelligent Activities:

Close the composing venture with intelligent activities. Scholars can investigate how their impression of the Normal Crackpot and its current circumstance have developed through their inventive articulations. This intelligent part adds profundity to the creative cycle.

7.3Prompts for further exploration of nature and wildlife in poetry

The universe of nature and untamed life offers writers a sweeping material rich with varieties, surfaces, and stories ready to be told. Verse, as a medium, has the special capacity to catch the embodiment of the normal world, from the sensitive complexities of a bloom's petal to the magnificence of a wild animal in its territory. In this aide, we'll dive into a variety of prompts intended to light wonderful motivation, welcoming journalists to leave on an excursion of investigation, perception, and emotive articulation inside the domain of nature and untamed life.

Observational Prompts:

Microcosmic Wonders:

Investigate the universe of microorganisms and small creatures frequently ignored in nature. Compose a sonnet that digs into the mind boggling subtleties of a blossom's life systems, the dance of bugs, or the secret life inside a lake.

Endured Scenes:

Catch the embodiment of scenes molded by climate and time. Portray the verse of downpour splashed fields, wind-etched mountains, or the cadenced dance of leaves during a tempest. Notice the effect of climate on the regular world and make an interpretation of it into stanza.

A Day in the Life:

Pick a particular day and narrative the everyday exercises of a specific animal, be it a bird, bug, or well evolved creature. Through your words, convey the schedules, difficulties, and snapshots of reprieve in the existence of the picked being.

Occasional Motivations:

Spring Arousing:

Create a sonnet that exemplifies the recharging and resurrection related with spring. Investigate the rise of new life, the blooming of blossoms, and the lively energy that pervades the normal world during this season.

Summer Song:

Wrap your verse in the glow and overflow of summer. Plunge into the tangible encounters of the time, from the humming of bugs to the sun-dappled scenes. Catch the sluggish, brilliant hours in refrain.

Pre-winter's Hug:

Investigate the topic of progress and change in harvest time. Expound on the changing shades of leaves, the relocation of birds, or the peaceful readiness of nature for the approaching winter. Utilize fall symbolism to bring out feeling and reflection.

Winter Murmurs:

Dive into the quieted magnificence of winter scenes. Expound on snow-shrouded scenes, the versatility of natural life in colder environments, or the peaceful quietness that covers the world. Embrace the distinct magnificence and thoughtful nature of winter.

Natural life Representations:

Creature Speculative chemistry:

Pick a particular creature and investigate its representative importance. Compose a sonnet that dives into the fanciful, social, or individual affiliations connected to the picked animal. Uncover the layers of importance implanted in the creature's presence.

Hunter and Prey:

Make a sonnet that looks at the sensitive harmony among hunters and prey in the normal world. Investigate the dance of endurance, the techniques utilized by the two trackers and the pursued, and the interconnectedness of species inside environments.

Imperiled Requiem:

Compose a sonnet that fills in as a funeral poem for a jeopardized or wiped out species. Utilize your words to catch the magnificence, uniqueness, and power of the animal's presence. This exercise can be a call to mindfulness and protection.

Ecological Reflections:

Human instinct Discoursed:

Make a sonnet that investigates the connection among mankind and nature. Utilize the refrains to ponder the effect of human exercises on the climate, the convergence of metropolitan and normal scenes, or the common encounters among people and natural life.

Eco-Nervousness Articulation:

Address the topic of eco-nervousness in verse. Expound on the difficulties looked by the normal world because of environmental change, deforestation, or contamination. Utilize your words to bring out a need to get a move, all things considered, or a source of inspiration.

Nature's Versatility:

Investigate the versatility of nature despite affliction. Make a sonnet that commends the regenerative force of biological systems, the capacity of plants and creatures to adjust, and the expectation implanted in the patterns of life regardless of natural difficulties.

Sensorial Investigations:

Scented Orchestra:

Jump into the olfactory universe of nature. Compose a sonnet that investigates the fragrances of various conditions — whether it's the hearty smell of a backwoods after downpour, the pungent tang of the ocean, or the sweet scent of sprouting blossoms.

An Ensemble of Sounds:

Catch the hear-able embroidered artwork of nature in section. Investigate the musical beats of downpour, the chaos of a tropical rainforest, or the delicate stir of leaves. Utilize onomatopoeic language and clear portrayals to convey the hear-able wealth of the regular world.

Material Amazing quality:

Dig into the surfaces and material impressions of nature. Compose a sonnet that drenches perusers in the vibe of greenery covered rocks, the cool dash of a breeze, or the non-abrasiveness of creature fur. Pass the tactile experience on through the language of touch.

Inventive Structure and Construction:

Haiku Concordance:

Embrace the effortlessness of the haiku structure to distil the substance of nature into a compact three-line sonnet. Utilize this structure to catch transient minutes, occasional changes, or the magnificence of a solitary picture in the normal world.

Villanelle Varieties:

Explore different avenues regarding the organized type of a villanelle to investigate rehashed subjects or holds back. Create a sonnet that circles around a particular part of nature, permitting the rehashed lines to repeat the cyclic idea of the normal world.

Free Section Opportunity:

Embrace the opportunity of free section to allow your words to stream naturally. Compose a sonnet that mirrors the immediacy of nature, permitting the construction to imitate the capriciousness and variety saw as in nature.

Individual Reflection and Account:

Nature Journals:

Share individual accounts or recollections connected with nature. Compose a sonnet that portrays a critical experience, a snapshot of association, or an acknowledgment roused by the normal world. Inject your own encounters into the woven artwork of your verse.

Nature as Educator:

Ponder the illustrations nature bestows. Make a sonnet that investigates the insight intrinsic in regular cycles, the patterns of life, or the strength viewed as in nature. Utilize your sections to convey the significant experiences drawn from noticing the regular world.

Cooperative Activities and Local area Commitment:

Nature Coordinated efforts:

Start cooperative activities where writers and visual specialists combine efforts. Match nature-roused sonnets with relating visual portrayals, whether artworks, photos, or other creative mediums. This cooperative exertion can offer a multi-tactile encounter.

Local area Nature Difficulties:

Arrange people group difficulties where artists meet up to expound on unambiguous parts of nature. This aggregate exertion makes a common investigation of the normal world, encouraging a feeling of local area and brotherhood among scholars.

Chapter 8

Conclusion

Ends, however frequently consigned to the last sections of a piece, employ impressive impact over the peruser's view of the whole work. Basically, a decision goes about as a scholarly handshake, leaving an enduring engraving on the peruser's psyche. As we leave on this investigation of ends, it is basic to perceive their multi-layered nature and the different jobs they play in various sorts of composition.

II. The Motivation behind Ends

1. **Outline and Reiteration**
   One essential capability of an end is to distil the pith of the former substance. Whether it be a scholastic exposition, an examination paper, or a novel, the end gives a potential chance to gather the central issues and contentions. This course of synopsis supports building up the focal thoughts as well as helps the peruser hold and understand the data.

2. **Goal of Account Strings**
   In exploratory writing and narrating, ends act as the story's outcome, taking care of potential issues and settling clashes. This goal is significant for giving a feeling of conclusion to the peruser, leaving them fulfilled and satisfied.

3. **Convincing Conclusion**

In enticing composition, the determination is a basic point where the essayist gets the opportunity to have an enduring effect on the crowd. It is the last an open door to build up the fundamental contention, appeal to feelings, and urge the peruser to make a move or embrace a specific perspective.

III. Parts of a Successful End

1. **Rehashing of Proposition or Principal Thought**
   A solid decision regularly starts with a compact repetition of the proposal or

principal thought. This effectively helps the peruser to remember the center contention and supports the intelligence of the whole piece.

2. **Synopsis of Central issues**

Following the repetition, the determination ought to give a brief outline of the central matters or contentions introduced in the body of the work. This builds up the focal thoughts and cements the peruser's comprehension.

3. **Combination of Thoughts**

A viable end goes past simple redundancy; it incorporates the different thoughts and contentions introduced all through the text. This blend features the inter-connectedness of the substance as well as raises the decision to a more significant level of scholarly commitment.

4. **Source of inspiration or Suggestion**

In enticing composition, a convincing decision frequently incorporates a source of inspiration or investigates the more extensive ramifications of the introduced thoughts. This urges the peruser to consider the meaning of the substance and, at times, propels them to make explicit strides or embrace a specific position.

5. **Shutting Comments**

The end comments of an end ought to be made with accuracy. Whether it's an interesting assertion, an essential statement, or a reflection on the more extensive ramifications of the point, these last words have an enduring impact on the peruser.

IV. Procedures for Making Effective Ends

1. **Staying away from Presentation Reiteration**

While an end ought to attach back to the presentation, keeping away from simple repetition is fundamental. All things being equal, endeavor to offer a new viewpoint or knowledge that expands on the basis laid in the initial passages.

2. **Keeping up with Consistency in Tone**

Consistency in tone is vital all through a piece of composing, and this turns out as expected for ends. The tone ought to line up with the general state of mind and reason for the work, guaranteeing a consistent change from the body to the end.

3. **Consolidating a Significant Citation**

A very much picked citation can add profundity and power to an end. Whether it's a line from a scholarly work, a verifiable figure, or a contemporary master, a statement can intensify the effect of the finishing up comments.

4. **Inciting Thought and Reflection**

A compelling end ought to wait in the peruser's psyche, provoking idea and reflection. This can be accomplished by suggesting logical conversation starters, testing suppositions, or presenting new points of view that welcome the peruser to think about the more extensive ramifications of the examined subjects.

5. Creating a Significant Shutting Sentence

The end sentence of a determination is an amazing asset. Creating a sentence that is both essential and significant guarantees that the peruser's last impression is one that resounds long after they have gotten done with perusing.

V. Ends Across Various Types

1. **Scholastic Composition**

   In scholastic composition, ends are fundamental to the construction of articles and examination papers. They give a space to blending discoveries, examining the ramifications of the examination, and recommending roads for future investigation.

2. **Experimental writing**

   In the domain of experimental writing, ends act as the summit of the account curve. Whether it's a brief tale, novel, or sonnet, the end is the writer's last brushstroke, forming the peruser's close to home reaction and by and large translation of the work.

3. **Powerful Composition**

In powerful composition, the decision is an essential point for building up the essayist's position and persuading the peruser to make a move. It is the last an open door to present a convincing defense and have an enduring effect.

VI. Normal Entanglements to Stay away from

1. **Presenting New Data**

   One normal misstep in making ends is presenting new data. An end isn't the spot to divulge new contentions or thoughts; all things considered, it ought to integrate and restate the current substance.

2. **Excessively Unexpected Endings**

   Ends shouldn't end suddenly, leaving the peruser feeling muddled. A very much created determination gives a smooth arrival, directing the peruser to a wonderful goal.

3. **Over the top Reiteration**

   While reiteration of central issues is fundamental for building up thoughts, unreasonable redundancy can prompt dullness. Make progress toward an equilibrium that builds up without being repetitive.

4. **Absence of Conclusion in Account Composing**

In exploratory writing, an absence of conclusion can leave the peruser unsatisfied. All story strings ought to be sufficiently made plans to give a feeling of culmination.

VII. End in the Computerized Age

In the computerized age, where capacities to focus are more limited, the significance of a convincing end is uplifted. Perusers, immersed with data, look for lucidity and reverberation in the end snapshots of a piece. Scholars should adjust their decisions to fulfill the needs of an undeniably advanced and speedy crowd.

VIII. Future Patterns in Ends

As composing advances and new types of correspondence arise, the idea of ends might go through changes. Whether it's the joining of mixed media components, intelligent components, or new story structures, the eventual fate of ends holds invigorating potential outcomes.

IX. Decision: A Summit and a Beginning

All in all, the demonstration of finishing up a piece of composing is both a zenith and a beginning. It denotes the finish of an excursion through the text while at the same time making the way for additional thought and talk. The specialty of creating a significant end lies in the capacity to combine, resound, and make a permanent imprint on the peruser's psyche. As journalists, we should embrace the decision as a useful asset, employing it with artfulness to shape the peruser's insight and inspire an enduring effect. In the steadily developing scene of composed correspondence, the determination stays an immortal and crucial component, overcoming any issues between the composed word and the peruser's translation.

8.1 Summarizing key insights from the exploration of the Common Loon in poetry

The Normal Crackpot, an animal of nature's effortlessness and secret, has long charmed the minds of writers. This avian species, with its eerie calls and unmistakable appearance, fills in as a wonderful dream, moving sections that investigate topics of isolation, flexibility, and the interconnectedness of the normal world. This investigation digs into the rich embroidery of verse devoted to the Normal Nut case, revealing key bits of knowledge into how this cryptic bird has been deified in refrain.

II. The Appeal of the Normal Crackpot in Verse

1. **Imagery of Isolation**

   The Normal Crackpot, frequently tracked down in distant lakes and lush scenes, turns into an image of isolation in verse. Writers regularly portray the crackpot as a lone figure floating across still waters, repeating the human experience of looking for comfort in the quietude of nature. The crackpot's frightful calls add to this feeling of isolation, making an air of examination and contemplation in graceful works.

2. **Style Moving**

   The actual magnificence and effortlessness of the Normal Crackpot are repetitive topics in verse. Artists paint striking pictures of the crackpot's smooth, highly contrasting plumage and its talented jumps into the profundities of lakes. The musical developments of the nut case become a wellspring of motivation,

with writers involving its tastefulness as a similitude for the fragile dance of life
and nature.

3. **Strength in Difficulty**

The Normal Nut case faces various difficulties in its natural surroundings, including
ecological changes and human infringement. Artists frequently draw matches between
the crackpot's flexibility and the human soul's capacity to get through difficulty. From
the perspective of verse, the crackpot turns into an image of solidarity and endurance,
exploring the intricacies of climate with a determination reverberates with perusers.

III. Beautiful Styles and Structures

1. **Symbolism Rich Portrayals**
   Artists utilize striking symbolism to rejuvenate the Normal Crackpot on the
   page. Depictions of its plumage, the gleaming lakes it calls home, and the
   ethereal nature of its calls transport perusers to the core of the nut case's territory. This tangible rich methodology permits writers to make a multisensory
   experience, drenching the crowd in the realm of the Normal Nut case.

2. **Similitudes and Imagery**
   Allegories and imagery are strong devices in the writer's weapons store while
   investigating the Normal Crackpot. The nut case's frightful calls might be
   compared to sorrowful songs or the murmurs of the breeze, adding layers of
   significance to its vocalizations. The nut case itself can turn into a similitude for
   different parts of the human condition, from isolation to strength, offering a
   material for writers to investigate significant subjects.

3. **Organized Structures and Free Refrain**

Verse committed to the Normal Crackpot traverses a range of structures, from
organized rhyme plans and meters to free section. A few writers settle on the discipline
of conventional structures, utilizing rhyme and meter to inspire a feeling of request
that differences with the wild, untamed nature of the nut case. Others embrace free
refrain, permitting the cadence and stream of language to reflect the smoothness of
the nut case's developments.

IV. Conspicuous Instances of Normal Nut case Verse

1. **"Crackpot Country" by Mary Oliver**
   Mary Oliver, celebrated for her sharp perceptions of nature, wrote "Crackpot
   Country," a sonnet that catches the embodiment of the Normal Nut case.
   Oliver's language is both suggestive and exact, illustrating the crackpot's reality.
   The sonnet investigates subjects of secret and association, welcoming perusers
   to examine the nut case's importance in the stupendous woven artwork of
   presence.

2. **"The Crackpot's Cry" by Wendell Berry**
   Wendell Berry, known for his agrarian verse, wanders into the domain of the Normal Crackpot with "The Nut case's Cry." This sonnet dives into the interconnectedness of every single living thing, involving the nut case's cry as an illustration for the more extensive orchestra of nature. Berry's work mirrors a profound environmental cognizance, entwining the destiny of the crackpot with the fate of the whole biological system.

3. **"The Call of the Nut case" by Robert Administration**

Robert Administration, eminent for his account and melodious verse, catches the otherworldly nature of the Normal Crackpot in "The Call of the Nut case." Through musical stanzas, Administration conveys the appeal of the nut case's call and its effect on the human spirit. The sonnet investigates the extraordinary idea of the crackpot's cry, recommending an association between the regular world and the domains past.

V. The Convergence of Science and Verse

1. **Logical Precision in Depiction**
   While verse frequently mistreats language and representation, numerous sonnets committed to the Normal Crackpot show a guarantee to logical exactness. Artists, motivated by the bird's regular history, incorporate exact insights concerning its actual properties, living space, and ways of behaving. This crossing point of science and verse upgrades the credibility of the beautiful depiction, making a harmonious connection between verifiable precision and imaginative articulation.

2. **Ecological Backing Through Stanza**

A few writers utilize their refrains committed to the Normal Crackpot as a stage for natural support. By featuring the difficulties looked by nut case populaces, including territory misfortune and contamination, writers add to the more extensive discussion about protection and the effect of human exercises on the normal world. From the perspective of verse, ecological issues become strong stories that resound genuinely with perusers.

VI. The Advancing Job of Normal Crackpot Verse

1. **Social and Folkloric Importance**
   Notwithstanding its environmental and tasteful significance, the Normal Crackpot holds social importance in different social orders. A few writers attract on the crackpot's place legends and native practices, injecting their stanzas with layers of social significance. This adds profundity to the investigation of the Normal Crackpot in verse, associating the avian subject to more extensive human stories and customs.

2. Computerized Stages and Sight and sound Verse

As innovation propels, the introduction of Normal Crackpot verse advances. Advanced stages offer open doors for artists to consolidate sight and sound components, for example, sound accounts of crackpot calls or visual portrayals of their living spaces. These vivid encounters improve the crowd's commitment with the verse, making a multisensory investigation of the Normal Nut case.

8.2 Emphasizing the enduring connection between nature, poetry, and human experience

Nature, verse, and the human experience are entwined in a magnificent dance, each accomplice impacting and forming the others in an unending movement. This investigation digs into the persevering through association between nature, verse, and the human experience, disentangling the strings that mesh these components into the actual texture of our reality. From the heartfelt stanzas that commend the magnificence of the normal world to the thoughtful sonnets that test the profundities of human inclination, the collaboration among nature and verse fills in as an extension that interfaces us to the significant insights of our common presence.

II. Nature as Dream

1. **Motivations from the Regular World**
   Nature has for quite some time been a wellspring of motivation for writers. The magnificence of scenes, the complexities of verdure, and the consistently changing seasons offer a perpetual wellspring of allegories and images.
   Writers, receptive to the rhythms of the normal world, track down in its variety an impression of the human experience. From the perspective of nature, writers distil all inclusive bits of insight and ageless feelings.

2. **Heartfelt Articulations**
   Heartfelt verse, with its accentuation on the heavenly and the beautiful, frequently tracks down its dream in nature. Artists from the Heartfelt time, like Wordsworth and Coleridge, investigated the otherworldly magnificence of the normal world. Their stanzas, mixed with stunningness and miracle, commended the greatness of mountains, the serenity of lakes, and the calm stirring of leaves. Nature, in these sonnets, turns into a mirror that mirrors the profundities of human feelings, from happiness to despairing.

3. **Biological Mindfulness and Promotion**

In the contemporary time, verse has turned into a vehicle for natural mindfulness and backing. Artists, perceiving the delicacy of the normal world, utilize their sections to feature natural issues and the results of human activities. The association among nature and verse, when established in tasteful appreciation, presently stretches out to a feeling of obligation and stewardship. Through verse, a sympathetic scaffold is worked between the human experience and the prosperity of the planet.

III. The Language of Nature in Verse

1. **Imagery and Illustration**
   Verse fills in as an etymological material where the language of nature is painted with distinctive imagery and illustration. The stirring of leaves might turn into a murmured secret, the trip of a bird an illustration for opportunity, and a dusk a material painted with tones of goodbye. Nature's components are not simple items in beautiful works; they are images pervaded with layers of importance, welcoming perusers to investigate the more profound elements of the human experience.

2. **Representation and Sympathy**
   Artists frequently embody components of nature, crediting human characteristics to non-human elements. This representation encourages a feeling of sympathy, welcoming perusers to interface with the regular world on a close to home level. A stream may stream as well as convey the heaviness of recollections, and a tempest may seethe as well as express wild feelings. In this human methodology, nature turns into a mirror mirroring the human mind.

3. **Rhythms and Examples**

The intrinsic rhythms and examples of nature track down a partner in the organized types of verse. Whether through customary meters and rhyme plans or the free-streaming sections of free refrain, writers reflect the rhythm of waves, the heartbeat of the earth, and the patterns of life. This cadenced reverberation lays out a natural association between the deliberate pulsates of verse and the heartbeat of nature.

IV. Nature as a Wellspring of Intelligence and Reflection

1. **Examination and Thoughtful Topics**
   Verse frequently fills in as a vehicle for consideration and thoughtfulness. Nature, with its quietude and immortality, gives a setting to reflective subjects in verse. Writers, through refrains that reverberation the quietness of a woodland or the endlessness of the night sky, welcome perusers to stop, reflect, and track down comfort in the pondering hug of nature.

2. **Repeating Accounts**
   The repeating idea of the normal world — birth, development, rot, and restoration — tracks down reverberation in beautiful accounts. These repeating themes become similitudes for the human excursion, reflecting the periods of life, love, and misfortune. The evolving seasons, for instance, may represent the recurring pattern of feelings, offering perusers a focal point through which to see their own encounters inside the bigger setting of presence.

3. Nature as Instructor

Nature fills in as a quiet yet significant educator in verse. Through perceptions of the regular world, writers extricate illustrations about versatility, fleetingness, and the interconnectedness of every living thing. A tree, enduring tempests and seasons, turns into a demonstration of perseverance; a blossom, sprouting and shriveling, a similitude for the transient idea of magnificence. Along these lines, nature turns into an aide that gives shrewdness to those sensitive to its lessons.

V. Nature's Part in Mending and Reclamation

1. Helpful Nature Verse

The recuperating force of nature is a common subject in verse. Writers investigate the helpful impacts of submerging oneself in regular environmental factors, whether it be the quieting mood of sea waves, the stirring of leaves in a woodland, or the immeasurability of open skies. Nature, in these sections, turns into an emollient for the injuries of the human spirit, offering comfort, restoration, and a safe-haven for reflection.

2. Eco-Otherworldliness

Consolidating components of eco-otherworldliness, a few writers weave an association among nature and the consecrated. The regular world isn't just an actual scene yet additionally an otherworldly safe-haven, a domain where the heavenly is appeared in the excellence and multifaceted nature of creation. Verse turns into a vessel for communicating a feeling of veneration for nature, and in doing as such, it encourages an association between the natural and the heavenly inside the human experience.

VI. Advancing Points of view: Urbanization and Computerized Age

1. Metropolitan Nature and Substantial Wildernesses

As urbanization changes scenes, writers wrestle with the developing connection among nature and the human involvement with metropolitan settings. The substantial wildernesses of urban communities might miss the mark on breadth of unblemished wild, however writers track down magnificence and importance in the pockets of nature that continue in the midst of never-ending suburbia. The tweeting of birds in city parks and the strength of plants in substantial wildernesses become similitudes for nature's getting through presence despite human turn of events.

2. Computerized Nature and Augmented Realities

In the advanced age, the manner in which we experience nature has extended to incorporate virtual domains. Writers explore this new scene, investigating the crossing point among innovation and the normal world. Virtual encounters of nature, whether through computerized portrayals or augmented reality, brief writers to scrutinize the credibility of such experiences and contemplate the ramifications for the persevering through association among nature and the human experience.

VII. Verse as an Impression of the Aggregate Human Experience

1. **Shared Imagery and Paradigms**
   Certain components of nature, like trees, streams, and divine bodies, convey shared imagery and original importance across societies and ages. In verse, these common images become strings that wind around together the aggregate human experience. The moon, for example, may represent secret and female energy in one culture and thoughtfulness and change in another. Through shared imagery, nature in verse turns into an extension that associates different societies and times.

2. **All inclusive Subjects and Feelings**

The human experience, with its bunch feelings and widespread subjects, finds a mirror in the differed scenes and environments portrayed in verse. Love, misfortune, yearning, happiness, and the quest for importance are subjects that resound through both the human heart and the sections committed to nature.

Verse, in its investigation of these general viewpoints, turns into a vessel for communicating and figuring out the interconnectedness of the human involvement in the normal world.

8.3 Inviting readers to continue their poetic journey with a newfound appreciation for the Common Loon.

Set out on a beautiful odyssey through the domains of nature, as we welcome perusers to cross the charming scenes possessed by the Normal Nut case. This excursion rises above the conventional, digging into the magical appeal of this great bird that graces lakes and streams with its frightful calls and exquisite presence. As we explore the wonderful waters, we intend to develop a newly discovered appreciation for the Normal Crackpot, changing avian presence into a dream motivates thought, association, and an extending bond with the regular world.

II. Setting the Stage: The Normal Crackpot Divulged

Prior to diving into the verse, how about we familiarize ourselves with the Normal Nut case. Gavia immer, as it is experimentally known, is a striking waterbird that occupies northern lakes and streams. Wearing highly contrasting plumage, the crackpot has a supernatural delight that has dazzled the consideration of artists since forever ago. Its unpleasant calls, reverberating across quiet waters, add a secretive song to the embroidery of nature.

III. Verse as a Door to Association

1. **Arousing the Faculties**
   Verse is a medium that welcomes perusers to completely draw in their faculties. Through painstakingly made sections, artists inspire the sights, sounds, and impressions of the Normal Nut case's territory. Perusers, moved to the edge of tranquil lakes or in the midst of the stirring reeds, become members in a tangible encounter that rises above the limits of the page. The nut case's calls reverberation in the psyche, the gleaming water reflects in the creative mind, and the actual pith of the bird wakes up in the peruser's cognizance.

2. **Cultivating Sympathy Through Stanza**
   Verse is a vessel for compassion, permitting perusers to step into the universe of another being, whether human or avian. From the perspective of graceful investigation, the Normal Crackpot turns out to be in excess of an animal; it turns into a hero in the story of life. Perusers, directed by the sympathetic hand of the writer, gain a more profound comprehension of the nut case's presence — its flights, plunges, and the quiet minutes it spends drifting on intelligent waters. This compassionate association frames the bedrock of an extraordinary excursion.

3. **Conjuring the Soul of Interest**

Verse flashes interest, alluring perusers to investigate the subtleties of the Normal Nut case's way of behaving, living space, and imagery. The writer goes about as an aide, bringing up the complexities that could get away from an easygoing onlooker. From the examples in the crackpot's plumage to the biological jobs it plays, each idyllic line welcomes perusers to become curious eyewitnesses of the normal world. This interest, once lighted, turns into a light that enlightens the neglected corners of the avian scene.

IV. The Wonderful Woven artwork: Refrains Committed to the Normal Crackpot

1. **"Mourn of the Nut case"**
   In the eerie stanzas of "Regret of the Crackpot," the writer catches the spirit blending calls of the Normal Nut case as it crosses the still waters of a twilight lake. The melancholy song turns into a representation for the distresses and delights that reverberation through the human experience. The crackpot, a ghastly watchman of the evening, welcomes perusers to look into the profundities of their own feelings, recognizing the magnificence and despairing that coincide in the dance of presence.

   Extract:
   Nut case, your melody punctures the quiet,
   A distressed cry across the reflected lake,

Reverberations of old stories and concealed distresses,
Watchman of the evening, your song unfurls.

2. **"Wings of Reflection"**
"Wings of Reflection" takes off through the figurative wings of the Normal Crackpot, investigating the subject of contemplation and self-disclosure. The nut case's capacity to explore both above and underneath the water's surface turns into an image for the dualities inside the human soul — the noticeable and the covered up, the cognizant and the inner mind. This idyllic excursion urges perusers to embrace the profundities inside and take off higher than ever of mindfulness.

Portion:
Crackpot, with wings that cut the sky and plunge the profundities,
Show us the specialty of reflection, the dance of light and shadow,
Reveal the secret flows underneath the reflected surface,
As we investigate the tremendous breadth inside, directed by your wings.

3. **"Orchestra of Serenity"**

In "Ensemble of Tranquility," the writer coordinates an amicable mix of the Normal Crackpot's calls with the regular world, making an orchestra that resounds with serenity.

The serene scenes painted by the refrains welcome perusers to submerge themselves in the tranquil scenes possessed by the crackpot. The bird's job as a director of nature's ensemble highlights the interconnectedness of every single living thing, underlining the sensitive equilibrium that supports the world.

Portion:
Crackpot, director of the ensemble of peacefulness,
Your calls wind through the stirring leaves,
As wind and water participate in a divine two part harmony,
Nature's song, a medicine for the exhausted soul.

V. Welcoming Reflection: Beyond anything that can be put into words

1. **Journaling Prompts for Perusers**
As perusers cross the graceful scenes devoted to the Normal Nut case, they are welcome to set out on their own excursion of reflection. Journaling prompts, roused by the subjects investigated in the verse, give a compass to contemplation. Inquiries concerning special interactions to nature, snapshots of isolation, and the meaning of avian imagery guide perusers in articulating their considerations and sentiments. The demonstration of journaling turns into a vessel for making an interpretation of the lovely experience into an individual story.

2. **Imaginative Reactions: Craftsmanship and Articulation**
The challenge to draw in with the Normal Crackpot reaches out indeed.

Perusers are urged to answer imaginatively to the verse — whether through visual workmanship, photography, music, or different types of articulation. The crackpot turns into a dream, and each imaginative reaction adds a one of a kind brushstroke to the developing work of art enlivened by the avian excursion. This intuitive aspect changes the adding experience to a participatory festival of human expression.

3. **Virtual Nature Strolls and Soundscapes**

In the soul of advancement, perusers are welcome to investigate virtual nature strolls and arranged soundscapes that catch the embodiment of the Normal Nut case's living space. Online stages offer a vivid encounter, permitting perusers to observe the bird's developments, pay attention to its calls, and practically meander through the scenes that have roused writers. These virtual experiences overcome any issues between the computerized domain and the normal world, encouraging an association that rises above actual limits.

VI. Cultivating Natural Cognizance

1. **Instructive Assets on Normal Crackpots**
   To extend the comprehension of the Normal Crackpot and its environmental importance, perusers are urged to investigate instructive assets. These assets give bits of knowledge into the bird's science, natural surroundings necessities, and preservation status. By diving into the complexities of the nut case's life, perusers can foster an all encompassing appreciation for the avian species and gain consciousness of the natural difficulties it faces.

2. **Local area Commitment in Protection**

The lovely excursion with the Normal Crackpot reaches out past individual reflection to aggregate activity. Perusers are welcome to draw in with nearby preservation endeavors and add to the prosperity of crackpot populaces. Whether through supporting environment protection drives, partaking in resident science projects, or advancing mindfulness in their networks, perusers become stewards of the normal world, effectively adding to the preservation of the Normal Nut case and its living space.

VII. The Never-ending Reverberation: A Call to Save

As perusers close their lovely visit with the Normal Crackpot, they convey with them the refrains that have unfurled as well as a recently discovered appreciation for the interconnectedness of nature, verse, and the human experience. The charm of the crackpot's presence waits, reverberating in the openings of the psyche like a song that will not blur. In this closing section of the excursion, we issue a call to save, secure, and sustain the enchantment of the Normal Nut case.

1. **Saving the Environment**
   The protection of the Normal Crackpot and its territory is an aggregate liability. Perusers are asked to help preservation associations, partake in neighborhood drives, and supporter for the security of the biological systems that support the nut case. By understanding the fragile equilibrium of these conditions, people add to the more extensive exertion of safeguarding biodiversity and guaranteeing the progression of the nut case's eerie calls across ages.

2. **Promotion Through Workmanship and Verse**
   Craftsmanship has the ability to rouse change. Perusers, having navigated the domains of the Normal Crackpot through verse, are urged to become advocates for nature. Whether through making their own show-stoppers, putting together local area occasions, or sharing the verse that has contacted their spirits, people can involve innovative articulation as an impetus for natural mindfulness.
   The Normal Crackpot becomes a subject of beautiful investigation as well as an image of the more extensive basic to safeguard the planet.

3. **Tradition of Appreciation: Passing the Light**

As perusers develop a profound appreciation for the Normal Crackpot, they become torchbearers of the avian heritage. The information acquired, the feelings blended, and the associations manufactured during the lovely excursion become a heritage to be passed down to people in the future. By imparting a respect for nature and verse, perusers add to a social legacy that esteems the magnificence of the regular world and perceives the significant effect of words in cultivating ecological cognizance.